RULES OF CIVILITY

for the

21st Century,

from Cub
and
Boy Scouts
across America

edited by
Henry C. Wheelwright

endorsed by
Mrs. Robert E. Lee, IV
Regent, The Mount Vernon Ladies' Association

RULES OF CIVILITY

for the

21st Century,

from Cub and Boy Scouts

across America

edited by

Henry C. Wheelwright

illustrations by John C. Wallner

Stone Wall Press, Inc.

1241 30th Street, N.W.

Washington, D.C. 20007

Front and back cover photographs by King Laughlin
for the Mount Vernon Ladies' Association

Interior line illustrations by John C. Wallner

Permissions: Quotation from Ms. Sommers in
Section 29—Conscience, and her end note quotation is
reprinted with the permission of Simon & Schuster from
The War Against BOYS by Christina Hoff Sommers.
Copyright ©2000 by Christina Hoff Sommers

Printed in the United States of America

Published by Stone Wall Press, Inc.
1241 30th Street, N.W.
Washington, D.C. 20007

Library of Congress Control Number: 00-133489

ISBN 0-913276-62-6

Designed and typeset by AAH Graphics, Fort Valley, Virginia

This book is dedicated to
Josephine Wheelwright Rust

who unselfishly devoted the last ten years of her life to rebuilding **Wakefield or "Pope's Creek Plantation,"** George Washington's birthplace in Westmoreland County, Virginia, and restoring the Washington graveyard. Her tireless efforts succeeded in preserving this historic landmark in perpetuity by the National Park Service.

By viewing bricks and mortar we can reflect upon the early years of the father of our country, the Commander in Chief of our Continental Army, and our first President, George Washington.

The rules of civility copied out by young George Washington and presented in this book became the bricks that built this boy's character and stature. This enabled him to become the most admired and revered man in our young country.

Hopefully these new rules, established by young Cub and Boy Scouts, can be the bricks for the Youth of America to build character, compassion, and other noble attributes to develop leaders and leadership for the 21st century and for future generations.

Table of

Introduction 11

History of "Rules" of Civility 20

Editor's Note 23

1. Respect 27

2. Stature 31

3. Shocking Behavior 34

4. Impatience 36

5. Sanitation 38

6. Cleanliness 40

7. Personal Appearance 44

8. Etiquette 46

9. Sincerity 50

10. Privacy 52

11. Discretion 55

12. Deference 58

13. Pride/Arrogance 62

14. Diplomacy 64

15. Authority 66

16. Temper 68

17. Sense of Humor 70

Contents

18. Criticism 72

19. Civil Discourse and Gossip 75

20. Attire 78

21. Table Manners 81

22. Friendship & Keeping a Secret 86

23. Leadership 89

24. Communication 91

25. Acknowledgement 95

26. Brevity 98

27. Fairness 101

28. Wholesomeness 103

29. Conscience 106

30. Self Improvement 109

Mount Vernon—George Washington's Home . . 111

From the Mount Vernon Ladies' Association . . . 112

Scout Salute to George Washington 116

Acknowledgements 120

About the Editor 121

End Notes 122–123

Civility Workshop 124

The Final Word(s) 142

Introduction

AS THE 18TH CENTURY drew to a close in the new United States of America, cold, blustery and nasty weather spread across Virginia. As was his custom, George Washington took to his horse in the early morning hours to inspect his vast Mt. Vernon estate. On that fateful 13th day of December 1799 the temperature dropped to thirty degrees, bringing snow. He returned later in the day with a chill that turned into a cold that quickly worsened. During the night he could scarcely speak and had trouble breathing. Yet he did not bother his wife Martha to fetch help. The following morning the best doctors of the time attended to him and bled him profusely in efforts to bring him back to health during the day. After making sure that his will and estate were in order, George Washington quietly died in his bed on December 14, 1799 at the age of 67.

There are many similarities between the end of the 18th century, the end of the 19th century, and the recent end of the 20th century. At the end of George Washington's life, the new United States of America had just been formed after having won independence from Great Britain. Yet it was soon to be tested in the War of 1812. With breathtaking speed it expanded westward to the Pacific Ocean and our great country filled out during the 19th century. During the Gay 90s (1890s), steel began building large cities and tall buildings literally rose to the sky (skyscrapers). Meanwhile, railroads carried people, goods, and material to and from these cities.

The 20th century verified America's importance in world affairs. Exhausted by decimating losses in the War Between the States, our young country was slow to enter World War One, which claimed millions of young European men, an entire generation, and finally ended British world dominance. America's entry into this terrible war helped bring it to an end in 1919.

Advances in transportation (the automobile and the aeroplane), communication (the telephone), and medicine were spectacular. Dread diseases like polio were basically prevented. Highways connecting population centers allowed us to come and go as we pleased whenever we please. Some of our grandparents grew up in an automobile-free society; yet they were later able to look into a small box and see an American dance on the moon! Parents of other grandparents grew up as slaves.

As we enter the 21st century we can surf the Web, dance in cyberspace, and "visit" almost anywhere someone is "hooked up". Soon we will be able to speak in any language and it will be instantly translated into another. You can enjoy your *latte* in cyberspace cafes around the world. Successful commerce is e-commerce. It's the present and the future.

But just as storm clouds brewed in the early 1800s and 1900s, are we looking out to another world war of epic proportions (nuclear, chemical, biologic, economic)? And what of internal intranational problems of civil unrest—rampant crime, trashing cities and property, and the decline of law and order? Will declining morality and common incivility accelerate?

Only the future will tell.

Is there anything we can do to head off or ameliorate these "worst case" scenarios? Perhaps. Reflect on character and values and the truth. Our youngsters of today and leaders of tomorrow will have awesome power—and responsibilities.

It will be up to them to develop good values for the future. Many institutions that have long been taken for granted are now on very shaky grounds, in decline, and are even under attack. Marriage, family, religion, church, school, community, and even country (the armed forces are desperate for qualified recruits). "Hollywood" today is the purveyor of sex and violence. It sells. But what is more insidious is its bias—anti-male, anti-Roman Catholic Church, anti-military. In its haste to focus on injustices, it is quick to distort history, sensationalize these distortions in graphic detail, and trample on the truth to create a box office success. Video games and Internet entertainment are just as bad.

When the newly elected senator from Minnesota, a professional wrestler and radio talk show entertainer with a high school education, proclaims in a Playboy interview that "organized religion is a sham and a crutch for weak-minded people who need strength in numbers" and continues that "it tells people to go out and stick their noses in other people's business," is this the message that should be going out to influence boys of Minnesota, our country, and readers around the world?

What youth group is most appropriate to put forth values to lead our country into the 21st century? The Cub and Boy Scouts of America. The best historical point of reference is a youthful George Washington. Life in colonial Virginia was much different from today's, but there are also many situational similarities to George Washington's boyhood. It is worthwhile taking a look at George Washington's early years. Out of this came his "Code of Civility" at the end of his formal education. He went on to an occupation (surveying) to support his mother and siblings, a brilliant military career culminating in leading a small continental army over the British as Commander-in-Chief, and finally unanimous election as the first President of our country and republic.

George Washington was born on February 22, 1732—the son of a Virginia land owner and gentleman. By the time George was six he had four younger brothers and a sister by his mother, Mary Ball Washington. His father Augustine had nine children by two marriages (his stepmother had died and his father had remarried). Only two died, which was unusual considering sweltering summer weather, flies, vermin, and other unsanitary conditions. George had lived in three different homes during his first seven years. While living at Ferry Farm near Fredericksburg, George's mother had another daughter, Mildred, who died in 1740. When George was eleven, his father was named a trustee of Fredericksburg (which was enlarging beyond fifty acres!). On April 12, 1743, George Washington's father died rather suddenly.

For a time thereafter he lived with his stepbrother Augustine, who inherited Wakefield or Pope's Creek Plantation. His education with

Rev. Marye in Fredericksburg allowed him to write out his Rules of Civility which are placed next to Scout Rules of Civility in this book.

While modern American families don't have as many children as in colonial times, most babies in America grow up to lead a full life. Nevertheless, less than half of modern marriages now survive. There is an increasing trend for poor young girls to have random children without the benefit of marriage. Often the father simply disappears or is not known, and more and more children grow up with a single parent. According to the U.S. Bureau of the Census, in 1960 about 5.1 million American children lived only with their mother. By 1996 this number increased to more than 16 million. Nuclear families are now morphing to include half brothers and sisters and/or stepbrothers and sisters. Divorce is customary, and even small nuclear families and military families are forced to re-locate over and over again with job transfers and re-assignments.

Many youngsters of today have a common bond with the young George Washington: loss of a father, moving around from house to house, and many other siblings to associate with, contend with, care for, and even compete with. George also had a mother to provide for and care for—a responsibility not assumed by many boys nowadays. This should make George Washington's "precepts" even more relevant to many youngsters of today and shed a new light upon this important person in our nation's history. Whatever helped George Washington to pull himself up by the bootstraps, so-to-speak, should be all the more valuable and appropriate to many young people today—before they begin to wallow in disrespect, despair, and even drugs.

Civility and respect is where to start. Not to abuse yourself (and others) with tobacco, alcohol, and/or drugs. To perpetuate civility is to turn away from violence and strive for a brighter and happier future for the 21st century.

At a younger and younger age, boys are forced to make important, hard decisions whether to embrace civility and a positive attitude and lifestyle of self-improvement and adaptation to society, or to turn away to cynicism, negativity, abuse, and violence. Civility . . . or rudeness, disrespect, and selfishly uncontrolled anger. The perpetrators of the Columbine High massacre, the anarchists of Seattle, the skinheads of racial hatred, the brutality and violence of inner city gangs. All have reached the depths of despair in flaming down the wrong path. At the end of this path there is nothing to find but sudden death or lengthy jail time.

But how do you explain the unexplainable? A 13 year old seventh grader in Fort Gibson, Oklahoma was a straight A student, popular with his classmates, belonged to a teen Christian group and school organizations, and had a lot of friends. When asked why he decided to pull a handgun in front of his school before classes and randomly start shooting his classmates, he replied, "I don't know." This was about the same time in life when George Washington was writing his rules of civility. Perhaps if this young Oklahoma boy had been more concerned with carrying a younger or handicapped child's books or opening a door for a teacher, this tragedy would never have happened.

What about adults and parents? As we spend less and less time associating with, communicating with, and interacting with other people (to include our kids or kids in general) the more self-centered and less civil we become. Wise men currently point out that the greatest threat to our society and even civilization is the increasing isolation of the individual that culminates in aggressive and violent acts. The individual has ever-greater powers of destruction. Rather than concentrating our efforts on taking away guns and other vehicles of destruction, we should work to restore in people a sense of caring and community and especially civility.

Signs of Civility Lost make the news every day—road rage, wife beating, shooting your co-workers (boss or stockbroker), or simply inconveniencing thousands of other motorists at a traffic choke-point because you have a personal problem. "Kill the umpire" is no longer an idle threat. Threats against classmates and teachers and schools are not taken lightly. Already parents and spectators around the country must sign a "silence" pledge before attending school athletic contests. What is triumphing over Freedom of Speech? The loss of civility.

To find positive keys to restore civility in the future, a shining example from our American history is a good starting point. Why not challenge the youth of America to come up with their own rules of civility as George Washington had considered at their age before he left home for the frontier, manhood, fame and fortune? My first thoughts were to approach high schools, but this was met with bureaucratic and logistical problems.

Happily, the private organization (The Mount Vernon Ladies' Association) that cares for and operates George Washington's home and most visited national "home" in the country embraced and supported my ideas. Michael Quinn suggested that we focus on Cub and Boy Scouts. He contacted leaders of the National Capital Area Council of the Boy Scouts of America (the largest of some 360 scout councils). Plans were instigated to hold a camporee at Mount Vernon on Saturday, November 6, 1999. We put together a brochure inviting regional scouts to the camporee and to salute George Washington before the 200th anniversary of his death. Individually or as a unit, Scouts were asked to imagine themselves in George Washington's place at his age and at their age, to consider the challenges of the new millenium, and to help draft the Boy Scout Rules of Civility for the 21st Century. Scouts who submitted ten rules of civility and conducted one commemorative event in their communities would be eligible to purchase a George Washington patch. Suggested community commemorative events included designating a "George Washington Day" to honor the legacy of George Washington at school or community, flying a replica of Washington's flag at a public event, planting a tree to create a living memorial to Washington, creating a George Washington Bookshelf at school or library, or writing a letter to the editor of the local newspaper about George Washington's legacy to the nation.

If Scout units were unable to attend the Salute, they could create an appropriate commemorative item such as a poster, certificate, handcrafted item, banner, wreath, personal letter or proposed Rules of Civility with the unit's identification. This could be sent to "George Washington's Bicentennial" at Mt. Vernon. These were all placed at George Washington's tomb as part of the salute.

Of more far reaching importance, The National Capital Area Council invited all the other councils and Scouts across the country (about 3,500,000) to have their own camporees to Salute George Washington. About 100,000 brochures were printed to reach this audience. Besides funding these brochures, I also funded replicas of the special George Washington flag that he flew outside his tent during the Revolutionary War. Each camporee that met the requirements to have their own "Salute" received a handsome flag of white stars on a blue field. I felt proud to see George Washington's flag flying under "Old Glory" outside a post office in Haymarket, Virginia.

Special Cub and Boy Scout camporees to Salute George Washington were held around the country and George Washington was introduced or re-introduced to libraries, schools, community centers, and even churches. Thousands of Scout rules of civility were delivered to Mt. Vernon or through Scout channels and presented at the Mt. Vernon Camporee. Wreaths, artwork and handicrafts were placed at George Washington's grave to honor the father of our country. On November 6, 1999, 700 scouts and 300 scout leaders pitched their tents at Mt. Vernon and more than 1,300 additional scouts arrived from around the region to Salute George Washington, participate in various activities, and present their rules of civility for the 21st century. Following this three-day camporee, camporees around the country, and scout enthusiasm, at high noon on December 14, 1999, bells in schools, churches, and communities across our nation tolled to remember the passing of the Father of our Country 200 years earlier, and flags were lowered to half staff.

After a brief look at Rules of Civility, which go back to 1595, all of George Washington's rules are presented, mostly as he wrote them, with slight editing for ease of reading. These are occasionally broken up

17

and categorized for cohesion. Cub and Boy Scouts were asked to consider these rules and to come up with their own rules of civility, behavior, and conduct for the 21st century. A diligent cub pack from North Carolina had each scout focus on a topic of Washington's rules, and individual responses from 8 and 9 year olds were quite impressive. Many of these are included in this book. From well over 5,000 submissions, 200 rules have been selected for the year 2000. My credentials to pick and choose are my relationship to Augustine Washington, George Washington's father and his son and George Washington's older stepbrother, whom young George lived with for a time at Pope's Creek Plantation (Wakefield) after their father died when George was only eleven. After so many years I hope George Washington would be gracious enough to indulge a cousin.

Many of the Cub and Boy Scout Rules of Civility for the 21st Century reflect Washington's rules and historical rules (see the History chapter); some are pithy and even irreverent to include the carefree nature of youth and our casual times. All are thought provoking. Many of the rules submitted were very brief, overlap, and espouse the Scout mantra—*Don't lie . . . be trustworthy . . . help other people . . . etc.* Many deal with the problems and potholes of modern times—*road rage, computer use, respecting yourself, others, and the environment.* Also the proverbial *don't put frogs down girls' dresses.* Many important values are reflected here—about family, community, religion and faith, and a lot about ourselves. We have asked a lot from these kids (some as young as 8), and some of these answers are pearls to live by. These responses may not solve a lot of problems, but if some gently steer people down the right path, this endeavor will be successful.

So what about manners and etiquette and politeness? And what do rules of civility have to do about the tea in China? Foreigners noted that even though George Washington never traveled to Europe like his stepbrothers, he had the charm and poise and stature not only to be a diplomat but also to command attention and build a reputation. In the ruinous days of the War of 1812, while the British were pillaging and burning Washington, D.C. and our President's White House, an enraged American onlooker shouted to British Admiral George Cockburn—"If General Washington had been alive, you would not have gotten into this city so easily!"

"No, sir!" Cockburn retorted. "If General Washington had been president, we should never have thought of coming here." Building a reputation and leadership for the new millenium. It all starts with reflections upon George Washington, civility, and simply saying "please . . . thank you . . . after you, ma'am . . . no sir . . . excuse me . . . I'm sorry."

There are no "right" or "wrong" answers. What individual Scouts or packs or troops have come up with will live with these Scouts into the 21st century. Perhaps one of these Scouts will some day be Commander-in-Chief of our Armed Forces, or a Supreme Court Justice, or even President of the United States of America. Perhaps these rules and his rules will help him get there. Perhaps these rules will give us all direction and benefit to head down the proper road of civility for the 21st century.

In 1999 a national poll found that over half of all Americans believed that "getting kids off to the right start" should be the number one national priority. Why not start with civility? Hopefully these Rules of Civility and Scout submissions from kids for kids (and adults) will help.

Henry C. Wheelwright
Editor and Publisher

History of "Rules" of Civility

ALTHOUGH CUB AND BOY SCOUTS across America have reflected upon "Washington's" rules of civility and responded with their own rules for a new century and their future, this is not the first time boys and future leaders and monarchs have studied a Code of Civility as an important part of their formal education.

Rules of Civility and Behavior originated in a 1595 manuscript entitled *"Good Manners in Conversation between Men"* from the Jesuit College of *La Flèche* which was soon shared with other French Jesuit Colleges. Jesuits of that time were frequently entrusted to educate the youth of nobility, and manners were an important subject.

To reach a wider audience this "Good Manners" manuscript was translated into Latin by the Jesuit scholar Léonard Périn, who added new rules regarding table manners. In 1629 a German printer (Nitzmann) published this text in parallel columns of Latin, German, and Bohemian. A Spanish edition followed along with a French edition in 1638 in Paris and 1651 in Rouen. Thus, by the middle of the 17th century "good manners" in conversation and at table became available across European cultures.

The first English version of these rules of civility appeared in London in 1640 under the pseudonym "Francis Hawkins". This was titled *"Youth's Behaviour, or Decency in Conversation amongst men . . .".* After a 1646 edition, a 1652 English edition expanded to 170 rules. Various editions of these rules were published in London by 1672. Of note is a 1664 version of "Hawkins" containing a second part dealing with *"Conversation Amongst Women"* dedicated to the heiress of "Laurence Washington, Esq.". Inevitably, cross translations appeared in France, with subsequent translations back into English.

In colonial Virginia around 1745 a youthful George Washington (age 13 or 14) familiarized himself with one of these *Rules of Civility*. When George was eleven his father died suddenly. Soon thereafter he went to live with his stepbrother Augustine at the traditional family home, Wakefield or "Pope's Creek Plantation", in Westmoreland County. There he began his formal education of business, mathematics, and surveying, for it was important to find a profession to support his mother and siblings rather than preparing for William & Mary College.

George returned to "Ferry Farm" near Fredericksburg where his mother and younger siblings were living. She (and later George) inherited the property. Evidence suggests that George's formal instruction at that time was by the Rev. James Marye, Rector of St. George's Church in Fredericksburg. For several years George studied mathematics, classical languages, and deportment from Rev. Marye between visits to his stepbrother Lawrence at Little Hunting Creek Plantation (Mt. Vernon). Marye had been born and raised in Rouen and studied at the Jesuit College of Rouen. In 1726 he renounced the Catholic faith, fled to England, and took up Anglican orders of instruction. During his first year of study under Rev. Marye, George Washington studied *The Rules of Civility* and wrote down his short version, which is replicated with very light editing in this book. Shortly thereafter his formal education ended and he left for the frontier.

George Washington's workbook sat undisturbed for many years at Mt. Vernon. In the 1830s Jared Sparks used his text in his *Writings of Washington*. In 1888 Dr. J.M. Toner published *George Washington's Rules of Civility & Decent Behaviour in Company and Conversation*. This took a full look at the original text to include abbreviations, spellings, punctuation, and gaps. Two years later Moncure Conway came out with his important work, *George Washington's Rules of Civility* that identified most versions of the rules to their sources and the interrelationships between various editions. Conway concluded that a version of "Hawkins" was the basis for George Washington's manuscript. Additional Hawkins rules that have no basis in the French Maxims appear in sequence, while errors in Hawkins appear in the manuscript.

John T. Phillips,II has brought out (1999) his excellent *THE COMPLEAT GEORGE WASHINGTON SERIES. Vol. 1: George Washington's*

Rules of Civility Complete with the original French text and new French-to-English translations. (Available from Goose Creek Productions, Box 776, Leesburg, Virginia 20178.) This historical chapter is largely based on his important new insights. He concludes that several rules in George Washington's manuscript follow the French rendition rather than Hawkins. Surely Washington's instructor was familiar with a French language version of the rules, perhaps a much earlier edition.

Just as Nitzmann (1629) presented "Good Manners" in parallel columns, setting Périn's Latin alongside contemporary German and Bohemian, I have taken Washington's found version (Toner), and have set George Washington's rules next to appropriate Scout rules. Scouts have reflected upon the same rules in their youth as George Washington did in his time. Centuries and language and customs change, but elements of civility do not. That is the common thread in this book. Rules of civility are just as important for the 21st century as they were for the 18th (Washington), . . . or the 17th (Périn), or the 19th century (Conway). Is there a better youthful population to turn to than the Cub and Boy Scouts of America for rules of civility for the 21st century? And don't we ever need them!

Editor's Note

SEVERAL MODERN "RULES OF CIVILITY" books based upon young George Washington's rules exist and are commercially available. I have borrowed from Letitia Baldrige's version of GEORGE WASHINGTON'S *Rules of Civility & Decent Behaviour In Company and Conversation* (copyright 1989 by The Mount Vernon Ladies' Association). These are mostly the "Hawkins'" Rules that most probably were the basis for George Washington's writings, and hence are appropriate for this text. More accurately, the Mt. Vernon rules are the J.M. Toner rules (1888) that most closely assimilate George Washington's writings. I have edited very lightly to improve readability, but I have not disturbed the original flavor of the material. George Washington's original manuscript is preserved at the Library of Congress in Washington, D.C.

For the purpose of this book and to better juxtapose recent appropriate submissions from Cub and Boy Scouts, I have categorized the various rules into 30 appropriate sections. Each section focuses on an important aspect of civility that has been chosen for its timelessness. The last and 30th section is new and important to the Scouts and us all, but was not included in previous versions of "Rules". Each section is content appropriate and enhances easy reference. You can leisurely read straight through the entire book, or you can quickly turn to the section of interest. Furthermore, I have occasionally broken down original precepts into parts: first part (–1·2), second of two parts (–2·2), etc. While this may disturb the continuity of young George Washington's original rules, this allows the reader to easily focus upon a subject and find Washington's original "rule" along with appropriate Scout rules. At the end of each of Washington's precepts I have identified each of his 110 precepts by number for further reference.

Note that while Washington copied out 110 original precepts, I have decided to include about 5 to 10 Scout rules for each of the 30 sections (or 200 Scout rules for year 2000). Good round numbers. All of the Scout submissions have become the property of The Mount Vernon Ladies' Association, and they have been assigned to me for the purpose of this book. They are in my possession and are fully protected.

The "rules" and other information supplied by Cub and Boy Scouts are just that—material voluntarily supplied to Mount Vernon with the full and complete understanding that it becomes the property of The Mount Vernon Ladies' Association. Nothing in this book is endorsed or sanctioned or has anything to do, officially or unofficially, with The Cub or Boy Scouts of America.

The text will flow historically from "Hawkins"/Washington to the Scouts and will invite new rules by the reader for himself and the 21st century. In fact a Workbook notation will invite you the reader to write down your important rule(s) as well. The obvious format is to have each section/chapter display the original precepts followed by the appropriate Scout rules—preferably on the facing page. This would allow for a short book for easy reference as well as comfortable reading with large type and generous spacing. Further note that the most numerous "Washington" section is Table Manners. Going back in time, the evening meal with family and guests became an important social occasion. Actually, in Washington's time the daily feast was in the middle of the day. Chow time today is quite different, unless you are putting on the occasional formal dinner party for important guests and dignitaries (or your boss). At the end of the 16th century, Léonard Périn added an extensive section on table manners. Perhaps this had to do with poor table manners of the time—food fights, lack of proper eating utensils, even reports from Germany of heaving dog dung at one another between courses for entertainment. All other sections have equal or heavier weighting to Scout submissions, which is the purpose of this book.

Another purpose of this book is to use civility as linkage between the past, the present, and the future. Would gracious acts be just as civil 200 years ago as today, or will be tomorrow? Times and customs change. *O tempora, o mores!* (Cicero, 63 B.C.). Hence, I have added editorial comments that hopefully will add insights, perspective, and relevance. Different type settings will enable historical, current, and editorial to be clearly differentiated. I have tried to cite "pure" Scout submissions, but, on occasion, I have felt required to use the slightest editorial brush.

The challenge this book offers up to you, Dear Reader, is to come up with your own version, or definition, of civility, and even your own rules/standards—and examples. At the end of this book you will find a section called Civility Workshop, which will coax you to investigate and focus on civility for yourself. You can start by reflecting on George Washington's and the Scouts' rules of civility to form your own rules. Perhaps you can think of ways to put these rules to practice with those you see every day, or meet in cyberspace.

If this Civility Workshop is used in a group setting—school, church, camp, organization, the leader can ask volunteers to read their civility stories to the group without giving names. Nobody would be embarrassed or singled out, and the benefits would be there for everyone. The simple things in life that may not be so simple. Some things we take for granted, that perhaps we shouldn't. Sensitivities that unknowingly hurt people. Perhaps by learning something about others and getting along, you may learn more about yourself and how better to bump along in the crowded highways and byways of the 21st century.

If there is gender bias in this book, it is towards males. After all, this is a book written by boys for boys that reflects upon the boyhood of George Washington. Many boys today live with their mother and see little of their father or interact with responsible men. According to a July 2000 Associated Press story, only 14 percent of approximately 159,000 public elementary schoolteachers in California (also the national average) are men. So perhaps a male perspective is warranted. Yet, these rules and concepts certainly apply to females as well. Civility is gender-neutral!

As the 20th century comes to a close in the year-of-our-Lord 2000, the life of a beloved English teacher, Barry Grunow, was quickly snuffed out on the last day of school in Lake Worth, Florida. Nathaniel Brazill was a seventh-grade honor student with perfect attendance. He was a skinny boy who played the flute and loved to joke around. The assistant principal sent him home early for throwing water balloons in class. He returned with a gun, which he used to shoot and kill the popular teacher.

How do you explain such madness? Civility is the antithesis of rage. To find civility, rather than a weapon; that is the challenge, and how to instill it in others. Perspective, composure, decorum, empathy, responsibility. We all need to search and come up with our own answers for a civilized 21st century world—a world beyond locks and legislation, beyond marching. Have civilized conversations and communications with your parents and your kids and your teachers and your schoolmates and . . .

Henry C. Wheelwright, Editor
July, 2000

1 Respect

GEORGE WASHINGTON'S
Rules of Civility & Decent Behaviour In Company and Conversation:

> Every Action done in Company, ought to be with Some Sign of Respect, to those that are present. (1)

> Sleep not when others Speak, Sit not when others stand . . . (6–1·2)

> Show not yourself glad at the Misfortune of another though he were your enemy. (22)

> When you see a Crime punished, you may be inwardly pleased; but always show Pity to the Suffering Offender. (23)

> Tis ill manners to bid one more eminent than yourself be covered as well as not to do it to whom it's due. Likewise he that makes too much haste to put on his hat does not well, yet he ought to Put it on at the first, or at most the Second time of being asked. Now what is herein Spoken, of Qualification in behaviour in Saluting, ought also to be observed in taking of Place, and Sitting down for ceremonies without bounds is troublesome. (27)

> They that are in Dignity or in office have in all places Preceedency but whilst they are Young they ought to respect those that are their equals in Birth or other Qualitys, though they have no Publick charge. (33)

> Artificers & Persons of low Degree ought not to use many ceremonies to Lords, or Others of high Degree but Respect and highly Honour them, . . . (36–1·2)

Please note that Washington was concerned about excessive pomp towards kings and royal people in high places. He eventually helped determine and establish customs associated with the office of President that are still followed today. He was concerned that the President should not be equated with royalty and preferred "Mr. President" to "His Highness, the President of the United States of America, and Protector of their Liberties," which was favored by the Senate.

> Do not express Joy before one sick or in pain for that contrary Passion will aggravate his Misery. (43)

John T. Phillips, II in George Washington's Rules of Civility (1999) references "Francis Hawkins" Youth's Behavior, which he claims represents "nearly a dozen different editions" of rules for young English gentlemen by 1672. "Hawkins" adds to this precept that you should sympathize with the sick person's infirmities for this "seeming participation" will "afford a grateful easement." The editor is not so sure. In aboriginal societies, husbands experience acute labor pains while their wives are having babies.

> When you Speak of God or His Attributes, let it be Seriously & with Reverence. Honor and Obey your Natural Parents although they be Poor. (108)

Washington's father died when the boy was only 11, leaving him to care for his mother and four younger siblings. Washington's older brothers from his father's first marriage inherited the best properties. George Washington supported his mother throughout her long life. She died shortly after her eldest son was inaugurated as the first President of the United States of America in 1789.

1 Respect

CUB & BOY SCOUT *Rules of Civility for the 21st Century:*

➤ The first three of 10 Rules of Conduct for Modern Times:
   —If you don't have something good to say, don't say anything at all.
   —Respect others that you are around.
   —Always follow the "Golden Rule."
>   *Jeff Rice*
>   *Troop 362, Sweet Home, Oregon (Robert Rice, Scoutmaster)*

From thousands of Scout submissions from all of the United States of America, the most often to appear was "Follow the Golden Rule—Do unto others as you would have others do unto you.

➤ Always respect other peoples' property.
>   *Mike Song*
>   *Grand Canyon Council, 4 Peaks District, Pack 171, Den 2*
>   *Scottsdale, Arizona*

➤ In all that we say and do, remember to put God first, others second, and ourselves last.
>   *Alton Lackey*
>   *Cub Pack 240, Hickory, North Carolina*

➤ Be kind to others. Try not to hurt anyone physically. Try not to hurt anyone's feelings.
>   *Pack 5, Westmont, Illinois*

➤ Treat animals with respect.
>   *Pack 367, Palmer, Alaska*

➤ Have common Courtesy for pedestrians and other drivers.
>   *Troop 144, Oxford, Mississippi*

➤ To live together, help one another, and help someone who is hurt. Respect other people's things and respect the color of their skin. Be kind with other people, especially older people.
Miguel Ferranzas
Pack 610, San Fernando, California

➤ Stay strong in your own beliefs and respect other people's beliefs.
Cub Pack 496, McKinney, Texas

➤ Don't be prejudiced towards someone who is different.
Ryan Conner, Troop 104, Jackson, New Jersey

➤ Be happy with who you are.
Daniel Coleman, Troop 104, Jackson, New Jersey

2 | Stature

GEORGE WASHINGTON'S
Rules of Civility & Decent Behaviour in Company and Conversation

> When in Company, put not your Hands to any part of the Body, not usually Discovered. (2)

> Turn not your Back to others especially in Speaking, . . . (14–1·2)

> Let your Countenance be pleasant but in Serious Matters Somewhat grave. (19)

> The Gestures of the Body must be Suited to the discourse you are upon. (20)

> Let thy carriage be such as becomes a Man Grave Settled and attentive to that which is spoken. (87)

At six feet, three inches, George Washington was quite tall for a man of the 18th century and consequently quite imposing. Yet he impressed those he met with his strong yet calm dignity. His good posture obviously enhanced this image. The early 17th century Maximes (Léonard Périn) admonish that it is uncivil to stretch out your body by extending your arms (on the table) or to assume different postures (fidget around). This was not mentioned by George Washington but may have been omitted in the mid 17th century "Hawkins" translations in England available to Washington's teacher.

The French maxims cautioned that in being attentive you should not have to say—"What'd you say? How'd that happen? I don't understand." and other "similar foolish remarks". Modern listening enhancement devices prevent such embarrassments and impositions on the speaker. Nevertheless, you should give the person talking to you your full attention. The speaker, as well, should take into account the listener's age and frame of mind.

2 | Stature

Cub and Boy Scout Rules of Civility for the 21st Century

➤ Never put yourself down, and always keep trying—even if you feel like giving up.

> *Cody Rink*
> *Pack 240, Hickory, North Carolina*

(See the Sportsmanship Story in the Workshop Section at the end of this book)

➤ Don't ruin a good apology with a bad excuse.

> *Troop 232, Cary, North Carolina*

➤ Stand still while saying the Pledge of Allegiance and act like a Scout when in uniform.

> *Pack 1, Lewisboro, New York*

By extension, the Scouts mean that you should always respect the uniform you are wearing, for it is larger than you. Behave properly as a representative of your school (sports team uniform), your community (police or fire department uniform), and your country (military uniform).

➤ When you are dealt a hard blow in life, roll with the punch. Look for the bright side. There is always a little good even in the worst situations. Find the good and make the best of it. You learn from your own and others' mistakes.

> *Wolf Cub Pack 9, Busti, New York*

➤ In times of difficulty, face the challenge with the foundation of your faith to stand firm with bravery and honor.

> *Den 9, Pack 289, Thompson's Station, Tennessee*

➤ Be tough without being mean and be principled without being fanatic.

> *Troop 3, Smithfield, Virginia*

➤ Be courteous and polite in all circumstances, even when you seem to be the only one remembering good manners.

> *Anonymous scouts*

➤ Be trustworthy in all your actions and speech. Your reputation, good or bad, will precede you all your life.
    Anonymous scouts

3 | Shocking Behavior

GEORGE WASHINGTON'S
Rules of Civility & Decent Behaviour In Company and Conversation

> Show Nothing to your Friend that may affright him. (3)

> Put not off your Cloths in the presence of Others, nor go out your chamber half Drest (7)

The 17th century Maximes *elaborated on this precept. Besides hanging around the house in your night clothes, you shouldn't leave your bed in disorder. (Your room a mess.) It adds that even though you might have a servant to make your bed, you should still endeavor to cover your bed before you leave the room. Nocturnal emissions are unpleasant to all—down through the ages.*

> Reproach none for the Infirmities of Nature, nor Delight to put them that have in mind thereof. (21)

3 | Shocking Behavior

CUB AND BOY SCOUT
Rules of Civility for the 21st Century

➤ Never abuse someone physically or mentally.
> *Ryan Nell, Boy Scout*
> *Akron, Ohio*

➤ If you're about to do something mean to somebody else, stop and think about it first.
> *Weeblo Den*
> *Pack 273, Oak Park, California*

➤ Never throw up in public on purpose. Don't burp in public, and never let out a big "toot" in school.
> *Kelly Hampton, Cub Scout*

➤ If you are hanging around with someone and they do something mean, don't do something mean also.
If you get frustrated, don't do something bad.
> *Cub Pack 513, Seagrove, North Carolina*

➤ If someone does something to you, **don't plan** to get **revenge!**
> *Pack 792, Frederick, Maryland*

➤ Do not hit.
> *Pack 143, West Linn, Oregon*

➤ Make no vulgar suggestions.
> *T. Koval, Boy Scout*

➤ Make sure your actions are appropriate to the occasion.
> *Philip Lee, Boy Scout*
Don't embarrass yourself and ruin an occasion for others.

4 Impatience

GEORGE WASHINGTON'S
Rules of Civility & Decent Behaviour In Company and Conversation:

> In the Presence of Others Sing not to yourself with a humming Noise, nor Drum with your Fingers or Feet. (4)

> . . . Speak not when you Should hold your Peace, walk not when others Stop. (6–2·2)

The second part of the French 1617 Maximes expand on this precept. You should not speak when others are involved in conversation. In other words, do not interrupt. As far as walking alone is concerned, Périn makes an exception for those in authority such as a schoolteacher in a classroom. This was very astute. Consider television commercials for new automobiles with the salesman and others rushing about. To attract your attention, modern commercial spots utilize strobe lights and increased volume with the "hurry over" message.

> Shake not the head, Feet, or Legs rowl not the Eys lift not one eyebrow higher than the other wry not the mouth, . . . (12–1·2)

4 Impatience

CUB AND BOY SCOUT Rules of Civility for the 21st Century

➤ To make wise decisions, take the time to think things through before making hasty decisions.
Pack 661, Den 3, Marysville, California

➤ Before saying anything, consider if it is kind, true and necessary.
Pack and Troop 423, Phoenix, Arizona

➤ I will not demand my teacher's attention when others need individual attention more than I do.
Marcus Evan Wittig
Northern Nevada Scout Council

But this 6th grader brought attention to George Washington. When his troop's Senior Patrol Leader declined to present the George Washington infor-mation to the Troop, this young Scout decided to do it on his own. With permis-sion of Father William Nadeau, at noon on December 14, 1999, Marcus rang the bell at St. Gall Catholic Church for one minute in honor of George Washington. Initiative, leadership, civility.

➤ Don't interrupt someone else's phone call. Don't honk your car horn if you don't have to. Don't hog the bathroom.
Den 4, Pack 542, Munster, Indiana

➤ Take your time on the road. Five minutes early is not worth risking your life and someone else's.
Troop 457, Rockville, Maryland

Many different Scouts and Scout units presented many variations of "avoid road rage". They all boiled down to patience, understanding, and composure. Unfortunately we all face increasing 21st century "traffic" and inconvenience.

➤ Do not run away from someone who is talking.
Pack 143, West Linn, Oregon

➤ Don't talk when someone else is talking.
St. Michael's Pack 324, Lake Jackson, Texas

5 | Sanitation

GEORGE WASHINGTON'S
Rules of Civility & Decent Behaviour In Company and Conversation:

> If you Cough, Sneeze, Sigh, or Yawn, do it not Loud but Privately; and Speak not in your Yawning, but put Your handkercheif or Hand before your face and turn aside. (5)

> *With regard to yawning, the 17th century French Maximes caution against yawning, for it is a clear sign of a certain* dégoust *(weariness) with those about you. If you can't stop yawning, refrain from speaking while yawning and yawning with your mouth wide open. Press at your mouth (*la sagement*) tactfully or slightly turn away from your company. In 1890 Montcure Conway references the anonymous 1673 work*—in sneezing, not to shake the foundations of the house.

> . . . and bedew no mans face with your Spittle, by approaching too near him when you Speak (12–2·2)

> Kill no Vermin as Fleas, lice ticks &c in Sight of Others, if you See any filth or thick Spittle put your foot Dexteriously upon it if it be upon the Cloths of your Companions, Put it off privately, and if it be upon your own Cloths return Thanks to him who puts it off (13)

5 | Sanitation

CUB AND BOY SCOUT
Rules of Civility for the 21st Century

➤ Do not yell in someone's face.
> *James White (age 11)*
> *Pack 20, Springfield, Ohio*

➤ Don't talk with your mouth full, and don't cough in people's faces.
> *Cub Scouts from a Webelos Den.*

From the 18th to the 20th and on into the 21st century, airborne germs, viruses, and diseases can be easily transmitted.

6 | Cleanliness

GEORGE WASHINGTON'S
Rules of Civility & Decent Behaviour In Company and Conversation:

> Spit not in the Fire, nor Stoop low before it neither Put your Hands into the Flames to warm them, nor Set your Feet upon the Fire especially if there be meat before it (9)

Travel in 18th century America by horse and coach was rugged, and conditions at wayside taverns were rough and unsanitary. Sickness and disease were dreaded and shortened many lives. Note that rules of civility often go beyond manners and good citizenship to include seeking a full and wholesome life. Consider this precept as analogous to visiting the communal salad bar at your favorite restaurant.

> Shift not yourself in Sight of others nor Gnaw your nails (11)

Here again, aside from the unattractiveness of seeing someone chew on his nails, simple infections in the 18th century could have fatal results—similar to viruses in the 21st century.

> Keep your Nails clean and Short, also your Hands and Teeth Clean, yet without Showing any great Concern for them. (15)

Much has been made of George Washington's dental problems, especially reflected in Gilbert Stuart's famous 1796 portrait. Dental practice to include the fashioning of dentures was quite primitive in the 18th century—for those who could afford it. Washington soon replaced the uncomfortable dentures that have since caused such comment. The message here is to try not to draw attention to your personal discomfortures.

6 Cleanliness

CUB AND BOY SCOUT
Rules of Civility for the 21st Century

➤ Pick up after yourself, but don't flush things down the toilet.
Cub Scout Pack 38, Brick, New Jersey

➤ The six white horses in Washington's stables had their teeth brushed every morning on Washington's orders. Point of Interest.
Artie Bodenmiller, Boy Scout

➤ Clean up after yourself and your animals.
Den 3, Pack 97, Santa Monica, California

This pack donated a bookshelf at their school library to George Washington, and each Scout cleaned up his bookshelves at home and donated a book to the shelf, which had only "three or four" books on Washington for the entire school.

➤ Be certain that you clean up the messes that you have helped to make, literally and figuratively. Others should not be responsible for correcting your unfortunate predicaments.
Boy Scout Troop 26, Ames, Oklahoma

➤ Try to recycle everything that you use during the day such as containers, wrappers, bottles, and paper so that we won't pollute our beautiful country. This will help save our natural resources.
A Boy Scout Troop

➤ You should not pollute or litter.
Jacob Biscan
Den 2, Pack 542, Munster, Indiana

➤ One shall always leave an established campsite better than it was found and an unestablished campsite without a trace.
J.Messimore, Scout

This should be the golden rule of camping for the 21st century, to which should be added—and make sure all fire and embers are completely out.

➤ Wash your hands before preparing food.

Ken Hart, Boy Scout

Doctors concur that washing your hands keeps you away from cold and flu germs. You won't pass them on to others, either.

➤ If a fellow Scout has dandruff, head lice, or a bad hair day, inform him privately.

Troop 43, Tuscaloosa, Alabama

7 | Personal Appearance

GEORGE WASHINGTON'S
Rules of Civility & Decent Behaviour In Company and Conversation:

> Do not Puff up the Cheeks, Loll not out the tongue rub the hands or beard, thrust out the lips, or bite them or keep the lips too open or too Close (16)

> Run not in the Streets, neither go too slowly nor with Mouth open go not Shaking your Arms kick not the earth with your feet, go not upon the Toes, nor in a Dancing fashion. (53)

Along with most Virginia gentry, Washington loved dancing and happy social occasions, but this did not carry over to calling attention to yourself in public.

7 Personal Appearance

CUB AND BOY SCOUT
Rules of Civility for the 21st Century:

➤ Take pride in your appearance, but don't be vain about it. Bathe daily and keep your clothes clean.
> *Gregory Knight*
> *Pack 942, Winston Salem, North Carolina*

➤ Never judge a person for their appearance, but for their beauty within.
> *Webelo 2, Pack 330, Arundel, Maine*

➤ Don't wear clothing with foul language printed on it, or say bad words.
> *Cub Pack 24, New Freedom, Pennsylvania*

➤ Try to have the best first impression because they are always important.
> *Pack 164, Yorktown Heights, New York*

Perhaps this should read "Try to leave the best first impression, for it is very important." The first impression people get of you is your personal appearance.

➤ Don't chew gum like a cow!
> *Matt Bishop*
> *Pack 3702, Pleasant Grove, Utah*

It has been reported that Robert E. Lee expelled a student for showing up at his office for an appointment, chewing gum. Your personal appearance can show disrespect for yourself and towards others.

➤ Judge others by what they do, and not what they look like.
> *Boy Scout Lloyd Becker*
> *Troop 40, Medford, New York*

8 | Etiquette

GEORGE WASHINGTON'S
Rules of Civility & Decent Behaviour In Company and Conversation:

> When you Sit down, keep your Feet firm and Even, without putting one on the other or Crossing them (10)

While this is still appropriate for American gentlemen, it is appropriate for ladies to cross their legs. Customs differ in other countries and cultures, such as Thailand. To avoid embarrassments at international functions, you should inquire about appropriate courtesies and customs.

> In Pulling off your Hat to Persons of Distinction, as Noblemen, Justices, Churchmen &c make a Reverence, bowing more or less according to the Custom of the Better Bred, and Quality of the Person. Amongst your equals expect not always that they Should begin with you first, but to Pull off the Hat when there is no need is Affectation, in the Manner of Saluting and resaluting in words keep to the most usual custom. (26)

While deference to heredity has all but disappeared in America and is declining throughout the world, the custom of removing your hat while addressing our flag during the playing of our National Anthem continues along with a military salute to our country's flag.

A lengthy French Maxime on these matters advises that among polite people a compliment is the most proper salutation. It never hurts to say "you look fit" or "what a lovely dress." However, another maxim directs that time and place as well as age and personal differences should determine the custom of compliments. Among businessmen, compliments should be brief (see Section 26— Brevity).

> If any one come to Speak to you while you are Sitting Stand up tho he be your Inferior, and when you Present seats let it be to every one according to his Degree. (28)

> When you meet with one of Greater Quality than yourself, Stop, and

retire especially if it be at a Door or any Straight place to give way for him to Pass. (29)

For the 21st century, this sign of respect will extend to ladies, elders, the infirm, and guests.

> In walking the highest Place in most Countrys seems to be on the right hand. Therefore Place yourself on the left of him whom you desire to Honour: but if three walk together the middest Place is the most Honourable. The wall is usually given to the most worthy if two walk together (30)

A 21st century gentleman should take the outside to protect his lady from traffic spray, etc. In Europe it was customary to take the inside to protect the lady from garbage being heaved out of windows.

8 | Etiquette

CUB AND BOY SCOUT
Rules of Civility for the 21st Century:

➤ Ask permission before using something that isn't yours.
> *Blake Badders*
> *Pack 240, Hickory, North Carolina*

➤ When one stays or visits in someone else's house, he should not defile it in any way or risk insulting his host/hostess.
> *David Harris*
> *Pack 942, Winston Salem, North Carolina*

➤ Be certain that you ask only for that which you can not do without when you are visiting others. Allow them the opportunity to offer to you that which you would simply enjoy.
> *Troop 26, Ames, Oklahoma*

By extension, when you are invited out to dinner, be careful about ordering the most expensive item on the menu.

➤ Do Not:
—take control away from the person who is playing a video game. Wait until the controls are handed to you.
—Shout when you are writing e-mail by using capital letters.
—Call someone on the phone and then put them on hold because your "call waiting" is clicking.
—Shout or talk to someone when they are on the phone.
> *Gordie Thigpen*
> *Pack 1365, Lake Ridge, Virginia*

Gordie has established some basic 21st century rules of etiquette for communications and home entertainment.

➤ Remember the "Magic Words." Say "please" and "thank you."
> *Pack 36, Darien, Illinois*

Pack 340 from LaVergne, Tennessee adds a few more magic words of civility for the 21st century:

➤ "You're welcome."
  "Excuse me" or "pardon me."
  "Yes/no sir or ma'am."

➤ Show up on time for meetings and other appointments, and, in a
  group setting, raise your hand before you speak.
  Den 13, Pack 79, Plano, Texas

➤ Try to open doors for other people, and let your guests sit in the most
  comfortable chair. Leave enough hot water for the next person, and
  never put an empty water pitcher back in the fridge.
  Scout Micah Keeno

9 | Sincerity

GEORGE WASHINGTON'S
Rules of Civility & Decent Behaviour In Company and Conversation:

> Be no Flatterer, neither Play with any that delights not to be Play'd Withal. (17)

> Superfluous Complements and all Affectation of Ceremonie are to be avoided, yet where due they are not to be neglected (25)

A "complement" is something that completes or makes perfect; a "compliment" is an expression of praise, commendation, or admiration. George Washington obviously meant "compliment". The same schoolboy mistakes occur today as appeared 250 years ago.

> In visiting the Sick, do not Presently play the Physicion if you be not Knowing therein (38)

18th century medicine was often very suspect, with several opinions frequently sought. This invited home cures and remedies, especially if a doctor could not be found. Resulting treatments were often perilous to a patient's health.

9 Sincerity

CUB AND BOY SCOUT Rules of Civility for the 21st Century:

> Spelling doesn't count, ever!
> *Brandon Lewis*
> *Troop 232, Cary, North Carolina*

> Don't judge others by how they look or what you have heard, but get to know them and make your decision based on the truth.
> *R. Leland Hernandez (age 9)*
> *Den 19, Troop 712, Dallas, Texas*

> When you feel you need someone to tell you they love you; tell them first.
> *Pack 328, Den 3, Temescal District, California*

> Admit when you are wrong and know when to forgive yourself.
> *Cub Pack 134, Brisbane, California*

> Don't say things like "Yeah", "Sure", "Whatever."
> *Pack 24, New Freedom, Pennsylvania*

> Always try to keep up impressions, for if you seem very nice the first time and you aren't the second they won't like you.
> *Tom Lipscomb*
> *Pack 164, Yorktown Heights, New York*

> Look thou into the eye of him with whom thou conversest.
> *Pack 149, West Linn, Oregon*

> Never tell a lie and you'll never have to remember what you said.
> *Robbie Barnett*
> *Troop 457, Rockville, Maryland*

> Be honest in all that you do and say. Honesty gains respect and trustworthiness from others.
> *Ron Barnett*
> *Troop 457, Rockville, Maryland*

10   Privacy

GEORGE WASHINGTON'S
Rules of Civility & Decent Behaviour In Company and Conversation:

> . . . Jog not the Table or Desk on which Another reads or writes, lean not upon any one (14–2·2)

> Read no Letters, Books or Papers in Company when there is a Necessity for the doing of it you must ask leave: come not near the Books or Writings of Another so as to read them unless desired or give your opinion of them unask'd. Also look not nigh when another is writing a Letter. (18)

Obviously to be avoided is the rudeness of disregarding the person or people in your company. With modern cell phones and instant communication with people all over the world more care must be taken not to ignore or disturb those in your company with your private business.

> Be not immodest in urging your Friends to Discover a Secret (60)

In other words, don't urge your friends or classmates to uncover a secret or expose a private trust.

> Gaze not on the marks or blemishes of Others and ask not how they came. (71–1·2)

Our nation has been fortunate to not being involved in a major global war for half a century with attendant wounds and mutilations for many returning soldiers. This has always been a source of curiosity and fascination for boys, but a very private matter for wounded war veterans who do not want to talk about it and recall bad memories.

> Be not curious to know the Affairs of Others neither approach those that Speak in Private (81)

10 Privacy

CUB AND BOY SCOUT *Rules of Civility for the 21st Century*

➤ Do not use your employer's communications (telephones, voice mail, e-mail, etc.) for your own personal private matters. When sharing a computer system, do not open and read other users' files and e-mail without their knowledge and permission. Protect your own files from prying eyes with passwords.

> *John Turner*
> *Cub Pack 28, Franklin, Pennsylvania*

John should have added the importance of changing your password from time to time. Maintaining your privacy is the greatest personal challenge for the 21st century. What you say or order or withdraw from your bank can come back to haunt you. The national security of our country is dependent upon elaborate encryption technology. Successful businesses must protect their proprietary interests.

➤ Be proper by excusing bodily functions or doing them in private.

> *Den 6, Pack 727, Hacienda Heights, California*

➤ Respect each person's personal space. (Do not talk in someone's face, etc.) Do not eavesdrop on other people's conversations. Do not use your cellular phone in public places that would annoy others around you (restaurants, church, movies, etc.)

> *Scouts from Marcy, New York*

11 Discretion

GEORGE WASHINGTON'S
Rules of Civility & Decent Behaviour In Company and Conversation:

> Do not laugh too loud or too much at any Publick Spectacle. (24)

Young George Washington neglected to add the rest of this Precept from "Hawkins": . . . lest you cause yourself to be laughed at.

> Treat with men at fit Times about Business & Whisper not in the Company of Others (77)

> In Discoursing of things you Have heard Name not your Author always A Secret Discoverer not (79–2·2)

> When you deliver a matter do it without Passion & with Discretion, however mean ye Person be you do it too (83)

Besides George Washington's interpretation of "meanness," the French maxim advises you to display evenness with simple people as well as important people. Hence, you do not lose control of the situation. (Spit not in the fire, nor Stoop low before it . . . nor set your feet upon the fire . . . 9) see Section 6: Cleanliness

George Washington's 9th Precept taken from "Hawkins" fails to account fully for the lengthy 17th century French Maxime (17) which addresses "fire" in detail.

Besides cautioning not to put your foot over the fire, it has curiously added not to turn your back "in honest company." It would appear that this would prevent you from mistakenly insulting somebody by turning your back on him or her in an effort to warm up. Furthermore, one is admonished not to crowd in closer than others, for this is the privilege of rank (parents, officers, guests, etc.). This is the first hint of politely forming a line—whether to hail a taxi, see a movie, buy groceries, etc. In some orderly, civilized societies, people line up and wait their turn. Elsewhere, the strongest brutes muscle in first and people sometimes literally get trampled.

Finally, advice is given concerning tending to the fire (stirring or adding wood), which should be left to the person assigned to this task. Perhaps your host would prefer the fire to go out so guests can leave and he can retire for the evening. Perhaps attending to the fire shows more attention to the fire than to the conversation. As an aside, would you like somebody to come into your house and putter around with your personal belongings?

Bear in mind that gathering around the fire was common from the 19th century back thousands of years to the Ice Age and cave men. Aside from food and warmth, this has often been a social occasion. Even in the 21st century, there will be times when the power fails and the pizza can not be delivered.

11 Discretion

CUB AND BOY SCOUT
Rules of Civility for the 21st Century:

➤ Do not allow hate and jealousy to govern your actions.
   Act courteously in front of others, even if you don't want to.
   Mawat District
   Occoneechee Council, BSA, Durham, North Carolina

➤ When sitting, don't lean back on two legs. It shows you don't care
   about what is being said and could ruin a good chair.
   Boy Scout Troop 692, Ajo, Arizona

➤ Think before you speak
   —You may say something bad that you did not want to say.
   —You don't want to hurt someone's feelings.
   —You might say something that you can't take back.
   Pack 792, Frederick, Maryland

➤ Don't brag when your team wins.
   Pack 82, LaGrangeville, New York
   *And it goes without saying that you shouldn't whine or complain when your
   team loses.*

➤ Be quiet about offending matters, and don't make a fool of yourself.
   Troop 454, Rockville, Maryland

12 | Deference

GEORGE WASHINGTON'S
Rules of Civility & Decent Behaviour In Company and Conversation:

> At Play and at Fire its Good manners to give Place to the last Commer, . . . (8–1·2)

> If anyone far surpasses others, either in age, Estate, or Merit, yet would give Place to a meaner than himself in his own lodging or elsewhere the one ought not to except it. So he on the other part should not use much earnestness nor offer it above once or twice. (31)

> To one that is your equal, or not much inferior you are to give the cheif Place in your Lodging and he to who 'tis offered ought at first to refuse it but at the Second to accept though not without acknowledging his own unworthiness. (32)

George Washington's hospitality at Mount Vernon is noteworthy. He referred to his home as a "well resorted tavern" with strangers traveling north or south usually spending a day or two there. Washington recorded an incredible 423 visitors during 1785. In 1797 he noted his first dinner alone with Mrs. Washington in 20 years!

> It is good Manners to prefer them to whom we Speak before ourselves, especially if they be above us with whom in no Sort we ought to begin. (34)

Perhaps from this understanding came the expression "children should be seen and not heard" that has prevailed through the middle of the 20th century.

> In speaking to men of Quality do not lean nor Look them full in the Face, nor approach too near them at lest Keep a full Pace from them. (37)

Currently in Islamic cultures a stare is considered aggressive and a form of commitment, and in other societies the "evil eye" is feared and guarded against. In America, boys are taught to meet a person with a strong handshake and look the person straight in the eyes to create a good first impression.

> In walking up and Down in a House, only with One in Company if he be Greater than yourself, at the first give him the Right hand and Stop not till he does, and be not the first that turns, and when you do turn let it be with your face towards him, if he be a Man of Great Quality, walk not with him Cheek by Joul but Somewhat behind him; but yet in Such a Manner that he may easily Speak to you (57)

Even the dances of the 18th century were very formal and precise.

12 Deference

CUB AND BOY SCOUT
Rules of Civility for the 21st Century:

➤ Listen and Respect other peoples' opinions, because even though you
may be right, you could be wrong.
> *Zac Hege*
> *Pack 942, Winston Salem, North Carolina*

➤ When you first meet someone older than yourself, address them as
Mr.—— or Mrs.——until they invite you to do otherwise. In trying
to make your opinion known to someone older than yourself, do so
modestly as they will be more inclined to listen.
> *John Amedo*
> *Troop 16, Akron, Ohio*

➤ Don't talk back to your elders.
> *Pack 329, Limerick, Maine*

*Even as a young CEO of a technology company with older employees? Another
21st century challenge to civility.*

➤ Accept that our ideas are not the only ideas. Thoughtful dialogues
accomplish more than voices raised in anger.
> *Troop 3, Smithfield, Virginia*

➤ Do not make fun of other people. Our differences are what make our
country great.
> *Anonymous Cub Scouts*

➤ Be helpful to those with special needs.
> *Pack 3400, Kreamer, Pennsylvania*

➤ Be silent when others read.
> *Pack 149, West Linn, Oregon*

*In the 21st century it will be increasingly difficult to concentrate on one thing
at a time for any length of time. "Quality time" for yourself and with others
will be more and more precious.*

➤ Take off your hat when you greet someone or enter a building. Hold
the door for your elders and stay out of their way.

Den 10, Munster, Indiana

*Tipping your hat may seem old-fashioned in the 21st century. It used to be
chivalrous to open a door for a lady, but now with "equal rights", many
women would rather open the door and barge through first. The elderly and
handicapped still appreciate a certain deference, such as being given a seat on a
bus or subway.*

13 Pride/Arrogance

GEORGE WASHINGTON'S
Rules of Civility & Decent Behaviour In Company and Conversation:

> ... Those of high Degree ought to treat them (persons of low degree) with affibility and Courtesie, without Arrogancy (36–2·2)

> Undertake not to Teach your equal in the art himself Proffesses; it savours of arrogancy (41)

> Reprehend not the imperfections of others for that belongs to Parents Masters and Superiours (70)

> A Man ought not to value himself of his Atchievements, or rare Qualities of wit; much less of his riches Virtue or Kindred (63)

13 Pride/Arrogance

CUB AND BOY SCOUT
Rules of Civility for the 21st Century

➤ Learn about the flag that represents the United States of America and show it the respect it deserves.
Pack 132, Carmel, Indiana

➤ Be aware and celebrate the different cultures around you each and every day. Celebrate the freedom we enjoy to be able to live in such diversity. Enjoy the pleasure that the Fathers of our Country would express if they could see their United States of America now.
Anonymous Scouts

➤ When asked to do something, do it with a glad heart and thanksgiving. It will make the task easier, as well as fun. Whatever job you are given, do it as well as you can. It is better to do it right the first time, than to have to do it over again.
Ron Barnett, Boy Scout

➤ Everyone should take care of his daily responsibilities independently.
Pack 792, Frederick, Maryland

. . . And cheerfully with attention to doing the best you can without having to be told or reminded. Take pride in what you do, and don't make your little brother do it.

➤ Use proper diction and grammar. Also, keep yourself in good hygiene.
Troop 32, Bedington, West Virginia

Most scout submissions are reported verbatim to include misspellings and grammatical inaccuracies. This retains the original flavor. Nevertheless, we should all strive to maintain and uphold high standards of communication.

14 | Diplomacy

GEORGE WASHINGTON'S
Rules of Civility & Decent Behaviour In Company and Conversation:

> In Writing or Speaking, give to every Person his due Title According to his Degree & the Custom of the Place (39)

In the 18th century it was very important to acknowledge royalty appropriately. At the end of the 20th century there has been a proliferation in the awarding of doctoral degrees in many fields. It is appropriate to always refer to a medical doctor as "Doctor", but this title is no longer of common usage in other fields. You will never go wrong in addressing a former ambassador as Mr. Ambassador.

The French maxims add further clarification to this tricky business. When addressing people held in public esteem, the customs of the country and the degree of the person's dignity will govern the titles you give to them. This quaintly suggests that you avoid insulting them. This particular maxim gives good advice appropriate to the 21st century as it was to the 17th: when you have finished your correspondence, re-read it in order to correct mistakes before you send it off.

> Go not thither, where you know not, whether you Shall be Welcome or not. Give not Advice whth being Ask'd & when desired do it briefly (68)

> Make no Comparisons and if any of the Company be Commended for any brave act of Vertue, commend not another for the Same (78)

John Phillips,II has recently pointed out in his George Washington's Rules of Civility that the original French maxims refer to praising someone for any brave act or for his virtue. This typo had been carried forward in various editions of "Rules" from Washington's time to the present.

> Let thy ceremonies in Courtesie be proper to the Dignity of the place with whom thou conversest for it is absurd to act ye same with a Clown and a Prince (42)

14 Diplomacy

CUB AND BOY SCOUT
Rules of Civility for the 21st Century:

➤ Never interrupt someone who is reading, writing, or in deep thought.
>   *Jackson Nye*
>   *Pack 712, Dallas, Texas*

➤ Don't be nosy about other peoples' problems.
>   *Pack 38, Den 3, Brick, New Jersey*

➤ Don't bomb other countries.
>   *Jason Snow*
>   *Pack 743, Neshannock Township, Pennsylvania*

➤ Believe in the power of reason to influence public debate and the power of the spirit to change private lives.
>   *Troop 3, Smithfield, Virginia*

➤ If people need to do the same thing, take turns.
>   *Ryan Boucher (age 10), Cub Scout*

➤ Don't blame other people for your own faults and give advice, not commands.
>   *Pack 54, Palmyra, Virginia*

15 | Authority

GEORGE WASHINGTON'S
Rules of Civility & Decent Behaviour In Company and Conversation:

> Strive not with your Superiers in argument, but always Submit your Judgment to others with Modesty (40)

> Being to advise or reprehend any one, consider whether it ought to be in publick or in Private; presently, or at Some other time in what terms to do it & in reproving Shew no Sign of Cholar but do it with all Sweetness and Mildness (45)

Cholar *comes from the French* colère, *which means anger or irritation. At the end of the 20th century this precept becomes even more relevant; so that the one reproved does not return to your office with a dangerous weapon, or tries to exact some other revenge.*

> When your Superiours talk to any Body, hearken not, neither Speak nor Laugh (84)

By "hearken" George Washington means you should not eavesdrop. It is also discourteous to distract or interrupt.

15 Authority

CUB AND BOY SCOUT
Rules of Civility for the 21st Century:

➤ Don't disobey your parents.

Robert Hoever
Troop 104, Jackson, New Jersey

Many scouts cited the Commandment—"Honor your father and mother."
  After George Washington's army had defeated the British, George Washington's mother was asked how her son had become such a successful commander. She replied simply that she " . . . taught him to obey."

➤ Do not speak angrily toward those who are in authority.

Troop 327, Sanford, Maine

➤ Be obedient to those in authority—upholding the rules you disagree with as strongly as those you wholeheartedly agree with.

Anonymous scouts

➤ Don't run away. It is no fun when you lose your mom or dad.

Den 3, Pack 75, Riverside, California

Thousands of kids disappear each year. You can't solve an unpleasant situation by running away from it.

➤ When parents or teachers ask you to do something, do it right away and cheerfully.

A Webelos Scout
Pleasant Grove, Utah

16 Temper

GEORGE WASHINGTON'S
Rules of Civility & Decent Behaviour In Company and Conversation:

> When a man does all he can though it Succeeds not well blame not him that did it. (44)
>
> *(See Section 15—Precept 45)*

> Let your Conversation be without Malice or Envy, for 'tis a Sign of a Tractable and Commendable Nature: And in all Causes of Passion admit Reason to Govern (58)

> While you are talking, Point not with your Finger at him of Whom you Discourse nor Approach too near him at whom you talk especially to his face (76)
>
> *President Clinton pointed his finger on numerous occasions, even at the American public on national television while stating he did not have sex with "that" woman. A common retort in a heated contemporary argument is "Get out of my face!"*

16 Temper

CUB AND BOY SCOUT
Rules of Civility for the 21st Century:

➤ Control your temper.
Curtis Johnson, Troop 232, Cary, North Carolina

➤ It's better to walk away than throw the first punch.
Matthew Dobbins
Troop 16, Akron, Ohio

➤ If you must disagree, don't argue and don't fight. Don't yell at other people, especially if you know you are to blame for the problem at hand.
Pack 110, Fairborn, Ohio

According to a May 1, 2000 Associated Press story, people who become angry very easily are almost three times more likely to have a heart attack. This is according to a study by epidemiologist Janice Williams while at the University of North Carolina at Chapel Hill.

➤ Gentlemen do not:
—Yell at the umpire.
—Aim balls at other peoples' heads.
—Slam doors.
Den 6, Pack 149 , West Linn, Oregon

➤ Be slow to anger and quick to forgive.
Ken Hart, Boy Scout

The Y2000 book CUSS CONTROL: The Complete Book on How to Curb your Cussing (Three Rivers Press/Random House) by James V. O'Connor cites two important caveats in Chapter 12, The Hard Part: Controlling Anger: "1. If modern-day life makes us angrier than in previous years, the need for civility is greater. 2. Swearing intensifies anger and adds to incivility."

17 | Sense of Humor

GEORGE WASHINGTON'S
Rules of Civility & Decent Behaviour In Company and Conversation:

> Mock not nor Jest at anything of Importance break no Jest that are Sharp Biting, and if you Deliver any thing witty and Pleasant abstain from Laughing thereat yourself. (47)

The comparable French Maxime elaborates on joke telling. If you find the occasion for a joke, watch out lest it be sharp-biting or a joke that tears "like a dog." Witticisms (les bon-mots) *and repartee* (les rencontres) *should be gentle and to the point without exciting anyone (indignation). Your jokes should not reach the level of buffoonery* (celle des bouffons) *by evoking laughter by extravagant representations and indecent actions (swinging your arms or crawling around on the floor). If you are clever enough to make others laugh, don't laugh at your own joke.*

Another French Maxime (27) adds important advice—Do not play practical jokes on those who would be offended by them.

> Break not a Jest where none takes pleasure in mirth Laugh not aloud, nor at all without Occasion, deride no mans Misfortune, tho' there seem to be Some cause (64)

> Speak not injurious Words neither in Jest nor Earnest Scoff at none although they give Occasion (65)

A French maxim clarifies "injurious words" to include nicknames that might amuse others but offend the recipient.

17 Sense of Humor

CUB AND BOY SCOUT
Rules of Civility for the 21st Century:

➤ Never laugh at someone else's misfortune. Instead, do what you can to ease their anguish.
> *William Ore*
> *Troop 567, Eden, North Carolina*

➤ Know when something is funny and when to laugh. But also, know when something is not funny and when to stop.
> *Patrick Flynn (age 9)*
> *Pack 942, Winston Salem, North Carolina*

➤ Do not laugh at other people's expenses.
> *Mawat District, Occoneechee Council, BSA, Durham, North Carolina*

(Mrs. Malaprop was a character in Sheridan's popular 1775 humorous English play The Rivals. She was made famous for her misapplication of words. Hence we get the word malapropism.)

➤ Do not joke about serious things.
> *Dan Pennington*
> *Pack 34, Jackson, New Jersey*

➤ Stay away from sarcasm.
> *BSA Troop 287, Marietta, Georgia*

➤ If your lunch falls in the porta-potty, don't and I mean don't get it out and eat it. (Ewwww)
Don't eat in your tent as the little critters might come and carry you away to their secret hideout.
Most of all never use poison ivy as toilet paper as it just might itch.
> *Scout humor from Troop 24*

18 | Criticism

GEORGE WASHINGTON'S
Rules of Civility & Decent Behaviour In Company and Conversation:

> Wherein you reprove Another be unblameable yourself; for example is more prevalent than Precepts (48)

> Use no Reproachfull Language against any one neither Curse nor Revile (49)

> Reprehend not the imperfections of others, for that belongs to parents, masters, and superiors. (70)

According to the French maxim, you are permitted to show an aversion that you have conceived. It adds that at times you may give advantageous advice to those in the wrong.

> (Contradict not at every turn what others say.)

The French maxim adds an important extension to Washington's 87th precept—Do not constantly contradict others by contesting and saying "that's not so" or "as I have already said . . . ". Defer to others' opinions—especially in matters of little consequence.

18 Criticism

CUB AND BOY SCOUT
Rules of Civility for the 21st Century:

➤ Don't mock other people's disabilities.
Troop 372, Philadelphia, Pennsylvania

➤ When visiting people do not point out messiness or any thing else that might embarrass them.
Tyson Badders
Cub Pack 240, Hickory, North Carolina

➤ When talking to someone or listening, don't be disrespectful with your facial and body expressions.
Brent Vaden
Pack 942, Winston Salem, North Carolina

➤ Don't talk bad about what someone else is doing, if you are guilty of the same thing.
Troop 712, Dallas, Texas

➤ Take responsibility for your actions. Don't blame others.
Scout Steven Swacina
Pack 574, Lubbock, Texas

➤ Do not hold someone responsible for his weaknesses. Help him better himself.
Troop 1, Frankfort, New York

➤ Don't plug your ears when someone is telling you something you don't want to hear.
Pack 3702, Pleasant Grove, Utah
Even though it might be embarrassing, one should always listen for ways to improve oneself. Nobody is perfect.

❯ Don't cut someone else down to make yourself look good.
> *Robbie Barnett*
> *Troop 457, Rockville, Maryland*

❯ Do not criticize people offensively.
> *Philip Lee*
> *Troop 457, Rockville, Maryland*

❯ Try not to anger or humiliate others.
> *Chris Moran*
> *Troop 457, Rockville, Maryland*

19 | Civil Discourse and Gossip

GEORGE WASHINGTON'S
Rules of Civility & Decent Behaviour In Company and Conversation:

> Be not hasty to believe flying Reports to the Disparagement of any (50)

> *"Hawkins" adds—But let charity guide thy judgment until more certainty. For by this means thou securest his reputation and frees thy self of rashness.*

> Never express anything unbecoming, nor Act against ye Rules Moral before your inferiours (59)

> Utter not base and frivolous things amongst grave and Learn'd Men nor very Difficult Questians or Subjects, among the Ignorant or things hard to be believed, Stuff not your Discourse with Sentences amongst your Betters nor Equals (61)

19 | Civil Discourse and Gossip

CUB AND BOY SCOUT
Rules of Civility for the 21st Century:

➤ Remember that a foul mouth disrupts conversation.
> *Michael Mavretic*
> *Pack 334, Raleigh, North Carolina*

According to a Y2000 book Cuss Control: The Complete Book on How to Curb Your Cussing (Three Rivers Press/Random House) by James V. O'Connor, a retired Army officer, Americans are more foul mouthed than ever, and many do not regard their offensive language as a problem. He observes that swearing does damage to relationships, to the individual, and to our society in general. Mr. O'Connor is even running a "Cuss Control Academy" in Northbrook, Illinois.

➤ When two people are talking, you should not ask them what they are talking about. If you think they stopped because of you, ask them to keep talking.
> *Austin Conrad*
> *Pack 942, Winston Salem, North Carolina*

➤ Do not disturb someone who is talking to another person and do not disturb the person who is listening.
> *Patrick Bohanon*
> *Pack 942, Winston Salem, North Carolina*

In other words, don't interrupt, make noise, or fidget around.

➤ Don't speak poorly of those who are not present, or listen to those who do.
> *Austin Brandt*
> *Den 7, Pack 942, Winston Salem, North Carolina*

➤ Believe only what words come from the horse's mouth.
> *A Scout from Durham, North Carolina*

➤ Use good speech. Only a low-life or an uneducated fool uses profane or obscene words.

Troop 692, Ajo, Arizona

The use of obscene words not used in extreme anger certainly reflects poorly on the intellectual capabilities of the communicator and the inability to express oneself most effectively. Do you think the punishment of washing a child's mouth out with soap should carry over to the 21st century?

➤ Do not repeat what will come back to slap you in the face.

Troop 186, Three Rivers Council, Beaumont, Texas

➤ Only bring out good qualities about someone instead of gossiping behind his back.

Troop 323, Western Colorado Council

➤ Be courteous in conversation by giving our full attention to whoever is talking.

Pack 3786, Ventura County Council, Thousand Oaks, California

Give him your full attention by looking at him—not away, nor at somebody else who might be more interesting or more important.

➤ Do not be quick to believe or spread rumors that hurt others.

Pack 200, Yorktown, Virginia

20 | Attire

GEORGE WASHINGTON'S
Rules of Civility & Decent Behaviour In Company and Conversation:

> Wear not your Cloths, foul, unript or Dusty but See they be Brush'd once every day at least and take heed that you approach not to any uncleaness (51)

Life in 18th America was hard and rugged, even for the gentry. Travel was grueling and adventuresome. Yet the customs of the time required good clothes and even powdered wigs for social and official occasions. This conveyed a genteelness and respect for the company and the occasion.

> In your Apparel be Modest and endeavor to Accommodate Nature, rather than to procure Admiration keep to the fashion of your equals Such as are Civil and orderly with respect to Times and Places (52)

> Play not the Peacock, looking every where about you, to See if you be well Deck't, if your Shoes fit well if your Stockings Sit neatly, and Cloths handsomely. (54)

Washington had a very active childhood in Virginia and was imbued with a sense of practicality and a sense of urgency to get on with many matters at hand. Personal vanity displeased him. He wrote to his nephew Bushrod Washington—"Do not conceive that fine Clothes make fine Men, any more than fine feathers make fine Birds. A plain genteel dress is more admired and obtains more credit than lace and embroidery in the Eyes of the Judicious and sensible."

The comparable French maxim to this precept continues with some interesting suggestions:

Do not leave your room with your pen in your mouth or on your ear. *I can understand not appearing like a pirate with a pen (knife) in your mouth, but a pen on your ear may be necessary for practical purposes. If you have no pockets and must move about and take notes while carrying things, what are you going to do?*

Don't put flowers in your ears, cap, or hat.

(Unless you are a girl from San Francisco, as the song suggests.) In modern times this suggestion would probably extend to metal studs in unusual parts of the body. This brings to mind the line from Yankee Doodle Dandy—"stuck a feather in his hat and called it macaroni" along with the British impression of American colonialists as rustic yokels.

Finally some extensive advice on what to do with your handkerchief:

Don't carry your handkerchief in your hand or hanging from your mouth *(toothache?!)*

Or at your belt *(like a scalp?)*

Or under your armpit *(!)*

Not on your shoulder

Or hidden under your coat.

Put it in a place where it cannot be seen, but from where it can be easily drawn when needed (a pocket). Above all, don't offer it to anyone unless it is clean (tout blanc—*all white*) **or** *passably folded.*

Please note the modern British expression regarding handkerchiefs:

One is for show; one is for blow.

20 | Attire

CUB AND BOY SCOUT
Rules of Civility for the 21st Century:

➤ Do not use vulgar or suggestive language nor wear clothing that supports it.

Troop 144, Oxford, Mississippi

➤ Dress appropriately. Know that there are certain situations in which the clothing you choose to wear, or not wear, will be more important to others than it is to you. At these times, if not offensive to your own, respect the values of those you will be with.

Troop 26, Ames, Oklahoma

This is especially true when traveling to foreign countries with different traditions. In churches, mosques, or temples, head covering may be appropriate and shorts inappropriate. In our country, you should show respect when visiting God's house of worship by wearing a coat and tie or your best clean clothes.

➤ Remove your hat or cap when indoors, excepting only those religious or fraternal rituals requiring the participants to wear a specific head covering. Dress appropriately for all occasions or activities. If in doubt, call the organizers and ask what to wear.

Pack 28, Franklin, Pennsylvania

21 | Table Manners

GEORGE WASHINGTON'S
Rules of Civility & Decent Behaviour In Company and Conversation:

> Eat not in the Streets, nor in ye House, out of Season (55)

In the 21st century when time is precious and it is easy and convenient to grab a bite on the run or in your car, this precept is long outmoded.

> Speak not of doleful Things in Time of Mirth or at the Table; Speak not of Melancholy Things as Death and Wounds, and if others mention them Change if you can the Discourse . . . (62–1·2)

> Being Set at meat Scratch not neither Spit Cough or blow your Nose except there's a Necessity for it (90)

> Make no Shew of taking great Delight in your Victuals, Feed not with Greediness; cut your Bread with a knife, lean not on the Table, neither find fault with what you Eat (91)

According to Moncure Conway (1890), George Washington invited each guest at Mount Vernon to call for or select the wine for his meal. Especially at a modern restaurant, this takes the burden off the host of selecting the proper wine. The guest should defer, for fear of blowing the host's budget for the meal.

> Take no Salt or cut Bread with your Knife Greasy (92)

> Entertaining any one at table it is decent to present him with meat, Undertake not to help others undesired by ye master (93)

> If you Soak bread in the Sauce let it be no more than what you put in your Mouth at a time and blow not your broth at Table but Stay till Cools of it Self (94)

> Put not your meat to your Mouth with your Knife in your hand neither Spit forth the Stones of any fruit Pye upon a Dish nor Cast anything under the table (95).

Please note that customary eating utensils were rare at wayside taverns and gentlemen usually carried their own forks. It is not bad advice, even today, to carry your own fork or chopsticks, when anticipating a meal in uncivilized places with potentially unsanitary conditions.

One French maxim suggests that the stones of prunes, cherries, etc. should be discretely collected with the left hand and deposited on the edge of your plate.

Another suggests that bones, peel, wine and the like should not be thrown on the floor or under the table. You don't want to cause an accident or the host's dog to choke on a chicken bone.

> It's unbecoming to Stoop much to ones Meat Keep your fingers clean & when foul wipe them on a Corner of your Table Napkin. (96)

The custom of the finger bowl between courses to daintily clean your fingers and lips is gradually disappearing.

A maxim advises you not to lick your fingers, and particularly not to suck them with a loud noise.

> Put not another bit into your Mouth til the former be Swallowed let not your Morsels be too big for the Gowls. (97)

> Drink not nor talk with your mouth full neither Gaze about you while you are Drinking (98)

> Drink not too leisurely nor yet too hastily. Before and after Drinking wipe your Lips breath not then or Ever with too great a Noise, for its uncivil (99)

> Cleanse not your teeth with the Table Cloth Napkin Fork or Knife but if Others do it let it be done with a Pick Tooth (100)

Toothpicks are infrequently available at certain restaurants. The custom of discretely using a toothpick after the meal is common within certain Oriental cultures. The more modern practice of flossing in private at least once a day is said to reduce plaque and the subsequent possibility of stroke.

> Rince not your Mouth in the Presence of Others (101)

> It is out of use to call upon the Company often to Eat nor need you Drink to others every Time you Drink (102)

Frequent toasts are common at a Russian feast. During a Sicilian wedding reception it is customary for the groom to raise a glass with each well wisher. This brings into doubt the ability to consummate the marital obligation later that night.

> In Company of your Betters be not longer in eating than they are lay not your Arm but only your hand upon the table (103)

> It belongs to ye Chiefest in Company to unfold his Napkin and fall to Meat first, But he ought then to Begin in time & to Dispatch with Dexterity that ye Slowest may have time allowed him (104)

It is still proper to wait until the host begins before you do, and it is proper for the host to wait until all are served before he begins.

> Be not Angry at Table whatever happens & if you have reason to be so, shew it not but on a Cheerfull Countenance especially if there be Strangers for Good Humour makes one Dish of Meat a Feast.

If you find something truly upsetting, it is simplest to excuse yourself, gain composure in the wash room, and return to table and a different topic of conversation.

> Set not yourself at ye upper of ye Table but if it be your Due or that ye Master of ye house will have it So, Contend not, least you Should Trouble ye Company (106)

In other words, don't switch the place cards at a seated dinner to suit yourself.

> If others talk at Table be attentive but talk not with Meat in your Mouth (107)

Please bear in mind that the original "Good Manners in Conversation among Men" that originated in 1595 was altered by Jesuit scholar Léonard Périn in 1617 to include table manners. Necessary social gatherings at table explain these many precepts. In colonial Virginia in general and Mount Vernon in particular, many traveler/guests turned up for the elaborate mid-day dinner (see Section 12—Deference).

At the dawn of the 21st century, meals range from the expeditious—finger food, fast food, pick up, carry out, home delivery to "power" lunches and even breakfasts to elaborate diplomatic and social dinner parties. Proper "civil" table manners is expected accordingly.

Most modern child psychologists agree that the communal evening meal alleviates the tensions of the day and brings the family together.

21 Table Manners

CUB AND BOY SCOUT
Rules of Civility for the 21st Century:

> No slurping. Wipe your lips. Don't eat and talk at the same time. Eat slowly. Chew your food well before swallowing.
>> *Clayton Miller*
>> *Pack 942, Winston Salem, North Carolina*

> Say "May I be excused?" before leaving the table.
>> *Blake Badder*
>> *Pack 240, Hickory, North Carolina*

> Never allow anger to sit at your table.
>> *Michael Mavretic*
>> *Pack 334, Raleigh, North Carolina*

> Don't bite off more than you can chew. Do not slobber when eating, and never talk about disgusting things around people who are eating.
>> *Pack 445, London, Kentucky*

> Don't eat till all are served.
>> *Scout David Perry*
>> *Troop 402, Jersey City, New Jersey*

A civil hostess will say "Please go ahead and start" after first serving guests and there will not be a blessing. Guests will be sure to enjoy the hottest food.

> When you eat lunch in the cafeteria (or public fast food restaurant), pick up after yourself. Do not stick gum under tables or chairs. Wrap it up and throw it away.
>> *Pack 542, Munster, Indiana*

22 | Friendship & Keeping a Secret

GEORGE WASHINGTON'S
Rules of Civility & Decent Behaviour In Company and Conversation:

> Associate yourself with Men of good Quality if you Esteem your own Reputation; for 'tis better to be alone than in bad Company (56)

> *This precept is especially important today—to avoid gangs and drugs and cliques in school. Good people of good quality would include church groups and Cub and Boy Scouts.*

> . . . Tell not your Dreams, but to your intimate Friend (62–2·2)

> . . . What you may Speak in Secret to your Friend deliver not before others (71–2·2)

22 Friendship & Keeping a Secret

CUB AND BOY SCOUT
Rules of Civility for the 21st Century:

➤ If you wish the friendship of another, strive first to be a friend.
Troop 249, Phoenix, Arizona

➤ Don't abandon your friends when they are in need.
Troop 693, Alexandria, Virginia

➤ People will judge you by who your friends are. Make sure your friends are people you can be proud of.
Pack 312, Ontario, California

➤ Act in a friendly manner toward all. Your respect of others will provide a guide to those who forget that every meeting is a chance to make a firm friend.
Anonymous scouts

➤ Always be a friend to the friendless.
Pack 324, Morris, Illinois

➤ Choose your friends wisely. Make sure the people you spend your time with are trustworthy, kind hearted, good natured, and responsible. Do not keep company with thugs, thieves, drug dealers or the like, because you may follow in their footsteps.
Pack 138, Busti, New York

➤ Share, for that is the way to make friends. The more you let other people use something you want to use, the more likely they will be your friends. Try not to have something all to yourself, for then they will not play with you or hang out with you.
Pack 164, Yorktown Heights, New York

➤ Listen and think about the suggestions of your friends. Don't do crazy things that people tell you to do just to be their friend.
Pack 214, University Park, Maryland

➤ Always keep your promises. Always keep "good" secrets and know
when not to keep secrets (like when someone is in danger).
Pack 92, Suisun City, California

23 | Leadership

GEORGE WASHINGTON'S
Rules of Civility & Decent Behaviour In Company and Conversation:

> Be not froward but friendly and Courteous; the first to Salute hear and answer & be not Pensive when it's a time to converse (66)

> Detract not from others neither be excessive in Commanding (67)

*John Phillips II (George Washington's Rules of Civility) has recently pointed out that later renditions of George Washington's rules mistakenly cited "Commanding" rather than "**Commending**". The original French Maxims clearly counseled "moderation in your praises." Even with this important distinction, this is an important attribute of leadership.*

23 | Leadership

CUB AND BOY SCOUT
Rules of Civility for the 21st Century:

➤ Look for ways to be unique in what you bring to your life and the lives of others.

Troop 341, Pittsford, New York

➤ When you are under the leadership of others, listen closely to be certain you understand what they ask of you. In so much as you are able, accept their guidance and work together, following instruction, to accomplish the goals you share with them.

Troop 26, Ames, Oklahoma

Many are passed over for leadership promotions because they have not properly carried out orders. It is unfortunate when these orders were not properly understood. Needless to say, orders from superiors (and parents) should be carried out promptly and cheerfully. By doing so you will gain respect and responsibility.

➤ Be brave enough to stand up for what is right.

Troop 693, Alexandria, Virginia

➤ Ask no more of others than you would ask of yourself; lead by example. Lead by allowing others to take responsibility, and follow them by offering your full support—even if you would have done something else had you kept control.

Troop 654, Mount Vernon, Virginia

24 | Communication

GEORGE WASHINGTON'S
Rules of Civility & Decent Behaviour In Company and Conversation:

> . . . Affect not to Speak Louder than Ordinary (8–2·2)

John T. Phillips II observes that George Washington's teacher incorrectly followed "Hawkins" (1640) in confusing raising your voice with becoming over-exuberant at play and getting carried away with its excitements. Nevertheless, those that speak quietly and choose their words carefully are the most listened to.

> Speak not in an unknown Tongue in Company but in your own Language and that as those of Quality do and not as ye Vulgar; Sublime matters treat Seriously (72)

The Imperial Court of Russia conversed in French. Lingua Franca is still regarded as the diplomatic language in many places. In Canada the use of French or English has caused great controversy to include language police in French speaking Canada. In many areas of the United States the Spanish language is currently in common usage. Nevertheless, English is the official language of the United States of America and the most universally understood. It is obviously most beneficial to use the language most easily understood by those with whom you are addressing.

The corresponding French maxim cautions never to use a foreign language of which you are not knowledgeable and familiar, except in the rare instance when it is necessary to clarify your thoughts. A California friend of mine would deliver her "perfect" French in such a manner and pronunciation that would at best confuse the French listener. The maxim also advises you to speak in your native language with erudition and eloquence, not with vulgar street slang. Unfortunately, in the 21st century vulgar and improper language is becoming more commonly accepted—even in English departments.

> Think before you Speak pronounce not imperfectly nor bring out your Words too hastily but orderly and distinctly (73)

In the rapid fire, fast paced, high tech world of the 21st century, it is all the more important to speak clearly and distinctly.

> When Another Speaks be attentive your Self and disturb not the Audience. If any hesitate in his Words help him not nor Prompt him without desired. Interrupt him not, nor Answer him till his Speech be ended (74)

> In the midst of Discourse ask not of what one treateth but if you Perceive any Stop because of your coming you may well intreat him gently to Proceed: If a Person of Quality comes in while your Conversing it's handsome to Repeat what was said before (75)

> When your Superiours talk to any Body, hearken not, neither Speak nor Laugh (84)

24 Communication

CUB AND BOY SCOUT
Rules of Civility for the 21st Century:

➤ It is not polite to use profane language on your e-mails. When driving with a guest, do not talk on a cellular phone-unless requested to by your guest. Turn off your cellular phone while attending a movie or a play. Phone rings disturb other patrons.
Troop 100, Phoenix, Arizona

➤ Never send a computer virus to someone else.
Keep a vocabulary worthy of scouts or clergy.
Don't interrupt! When it's your turn to talk, e-mail it.
A Scout from Durham, North Carolina

➤ Internet:
—The internet is not a toy. You should not play on it.
—You should not yell at people over the e-mail by using capital letters for your message.
—Do not download without permission.
—Only look at e-mail addressed to you. You should never read someone else's mail.
—When in a chat room, do not give out personal details or insult people.
Pack 24, New Freedom, Pennsylvania
Several scouts also submitted the simple rule of "no spamming." Playing on the internet can get you in very serious trouble, especially if you pretend you are somebody else and make a threatening comment.

➤ Do not ask stupid questions or give stupid answers.
Submitted by 4th grade Cub Scouts

➤ Try to keep good lines of communication flowing with all those with whom you work. Let other "surprises" result only from changing circumstances, not because you failed to keep others well informed.
Troop 654, Mount Vernon, Virginia

Many important battles throughout history were lost because of miscommunications and communication failure. "Secure" (private) communication is an increasing challenge for the 21st century.

➤ Recognize that listening is a very good way of communicating.
          Troop 3, Smithfield, Virginia

25 Acknowledgement

GEORGE WASHINGTON'S
Rules of Civility & Decent Behaviour In Company and Conversation:

> Take all Admonitions thankfully in what Time or Place Soever given but afterwards not being culpable take a Time & Place convenient to let him know it that gave them. (46)

If you are warned about a particular person or situation to avoid, thank the giver of these admonitions. If you are cautioned about improper behavior or taking a particular course of action, report later to whoever was concerned.

It is common courtesy to personally thank your host before leaving a dinner or party. A thank you note should also be written or e-mailed for a gift received. A "bread and butter" note shows your appreciation for the effort your host has gone to for your benefit.

25 Acknowledgement.

CUB AND BOY SCOUT
Rules of Civility for the 21st Century:

➤ Congratulate others on doing a good job. Don't take away from others' glory. If someone does a good job, tell him or her. Don't say you can do it better.

Cub Scout Pack 101, Woodridge, Illinois

➤ Don't dwell on others' problems, but rather on their finer qualities.

A Scout from Durham, North Carolina

➤ When you do or say something wrong, say you are sorry.

Cub Pack 70, Hamilton & Kidder, Missouri

➤ Be willing to admit and apologize for your behavior, should it offend another. Then be sure to avoid repeating it! Express your appreciation for the actions of others that benefit you or those you care for. A word of thanks is never wasted—unless it is not spoken.

Troop 26, Ames, Oklahoma

➤ Have a grateful heart towards God, your leaders, your parents, and your country.

Scouts from a Troop 1649

And don't forget to thank your friends for being friends when you need them.

26 Brevity

GEORGE WASHINGTON'S
Rules of Civility & Decent Behaviour In Company and Conversation:

> Let your Discourse with Men of Business be short and comprehensive. (35)

> Be not Tedious in Discourse or in reading unless you find the Company pleased therewith (80)

> In Company of those of Higher Quality than yourself Speak not till you are ask'd a Question; then Stand upright put of your Hat & Answer in few Words (85)

This especially applies to elders and school masters.

> Be not tedious in Discourse, make not many Digressions, nor repeat often the Same manner of Discourse (88)

This has great practical value, not only in the military where concise timely information is important, but also for the Executive branch of our government. General and then President Dwight Eisenhower insisted that memos be less than a page. Vice President Al Gore issued a directive that intra-office correspondences utilize short, simple sentences with a simple vocabulary easily understood by all.

The comparable French maxim summarizes that you should be brief, particularly when the subject is of little importance, or if you recognize signs of boredom in your audience.

26 Brevity

CUB AND BOY SCOUT
Rules of Civility for the 21st Century:

> Do not go somewhere if you are not sure whether you are welcome. Don't be nosy, but if asked for advice, make it quick.
> > *Duke Campbell*
> > *Pack 942, Winston Salem, North Carolina*

> If you're full of bull, keep your mouth shut.
> > *A Scout from Troop 232, Cary, North Carolina*

> When meeting with others (especially if you are new to a group), focus on listening. Speak only if you are sure that what you will say will provide new perspectives or information to the discussion.
> > *Troop 654, Mount Vernon, Virginia*

> While speaking to others, keep it short and to the point.
> > *Scouts from Marcy, New York*

> When using a pay phone, if someone is waiting behind you, make your call brief.
> > *Pack 542, Munster, Indiana*

The difference between essential and non-essential information and communication becomes more and more relevant in our 21st century culture and society with time constraints. There are times when information must be conveyed quickly, briefly, and concisely; there are other quality times when haste is not a factor and you can expand your intellectual and creative capabilities to create a broader perspective and depth of understanding.

27 | Fairness

GEORGE WASHINGTON'S
Rules of Civility & Decent Behaviour In Company and Conversation:

> If two contend together take not the part of either unconstrained; and be not obstinate in your own Opinion, in Things indiferent be of the Major Side (69)

An 1887 work (Of Education) attributed to Obadiah Walker interprets this rule as to

> Thrust not yourself to be moderator or umpire in controversies, until required.

In other words, mind your own business. Majority rules exemplifies democratic process.

> In Disputes, be not So Desireous to Overcome as not to give Liberty to each one to deliver his Opinion and Submit to ye Judgment of ye Major Part especially if they are Judges of the Dispute (86)

Major Part = majority (rules). Democracy in action.

> Speak not Evil of the absent for it is unjust (89)

27 Fairness

CUB AND BOY SCOUT
Rules of Civility for the 21st Century:

➤ Look closely and carefully so that you can see more than one point of view.
> *Boy Scout Troop 341, Pittsford, New York*

➤ Play fair. Do not cheat.
> *Josiah Hill*
> *Den 8, Pack 340, Lavergne, Tennessee*

➤ Think about **what** is right, not **who** is right.
> *Pack 158, Jefferson, Georgia*

➤ Don't force people to do what they don't want to do.
> *Den 4, Pack 542, Munster, Indiana*

➤ Give a bully plenty of chances to stop bothering you before you fight back.
> *Scout Micah Keeno*

➤ Don't make anyone feel left out.
> *Scout Adam Arnesen*
> *Pleasant Grove, Utah*

➤ Do a day's work for a day's pay.
> *Scout Matt Petrocci*

28 | Wholesomeness

GEORGE WASHINGTON'S
Rules of Civility & Decent Behaviour In Company and Conversation:

> . . . Nor act against ye Rules Moral before your inferiours (59–2·2)

The most commonly submitted and universal precept of the Cub and Boy Scouts is to follow the Golden Rule—Do unto others as you would have them do unto you.

> Let your Recreations be Manfull not Sinfull.(109)

The Scouts stress the importance of a clean and healthy body and mind.

28 Wholesomeness

CUB AND BOY SCOUT
Rules of Civility for the 21st Century:

➤ Plant your mind with flowers, not weeds.
Troop 846, Independence, Missouri

➤ Show good sportsmanship in all areas of life; not just in sports.
Troop 567, Eden, North Carolina

➤ Avoid drugs in the politest manner.
A scout from Durham, North Carolina

➤ Maintain a cheerful disposition whenever it is appropriate.
Matthew Hege
Pack 942, Winston Salem, North Carolina

➤ Start each day with a smile.
Scout Josh Vidmar

➤ Don't waste time, but play a little every day.
Pack 134, Brisbane, California

Remember the old saying—"All work and no play makes Jack a dull boy."
Occasionally take the time to relax your brain and body and enjoy life. You
will be easier on yourself and more civil to others.

➤ Take not anything harmful into your body.
Troop 490, Orem, Utah

Aside from health considerations, certain cultures and religions frown upon the
use or consumption of tobacco, alcohol, meat, coffee, etc. A good host should be
aware of this and have appropriate alternative foods and beverages available.

➤ You should be reverent and listen to the talks at church. Say your
prayers every morning and night without being reminded.
Scout Spencer Arnesen (age 8)
Pleasant Grove, Utah

Another one of Spencer's rules may be the most difficult of all for youngsters to follow—You should clean up your room without being asked.

➤ Listen to music that is in good taste.

Troop 457, Rockville, Maryland

Some music has endured for decades and centuries for a reason. This precept also applies to books and visual entertainment. A civilized person of the 21st century should be concerned about standards, values, and improving yourself as a person.

➤ Leave places you visit better than you found them. Take care of the environment and all of God's creatures.

Scout Ken Hart

29 | Conscience

GEORGE WASHINGTON'S
Rules of Civility & Decent Behaviour In Company and Conversation:

> Labour to keep alive in your Breast that Little Spark of Celestial fire Called Conscience. (110)

According to modern psychologists, "conscience" takes hold in the first few years of life. My friend Barbara Hines has mentioned the importance of a consistent, nurturing caretaker and caregiver who is interactive and hands-on with the new baby. Of greatest importance is a deep love with no strings attached to develop a conscience in the young child. If this love is betrayed, compromised, or destroyed, "conscience" in the young child will be destroyed.

The importance of a father to a young boy is profound. Christina Hoff Sommers in The War Against BOYS, How Misguided Feminism is harming our Young Men (Simon and Schuster, 2000) references a paper by Cynthia Harper (University of Pennsylvania) and Sara McLanahan (Princeton) "Father Abuse and Youth Incarceration" presented to the American Sociological Association in 1998. From a population (adjusted for race, income, and parents' education) of 6,000 males age 14–22 between 1979 and 1993, boys from fatherless homes were twice as likely to have spent time in jail. To quote Ms. Sommers: "Fathers appear to be central in helping sons develop a conscience and a sense of responsible manhood . . . Fathers play an indispensable civilizing role in the social ecosystem; therefore, fewer fathers, more male violence."

Since George Washington lost his father when he was eleven, surely this, his last precept, was important to him.

29 Conscience

CUB AND BOY SCOUT
Rules of Civility for the 21st Century:

➤ Do not follow the path of others when you know it is wrong.
> *Matthew Dobbins*
> *Troop 16, Akron, Ohio*

➤ Always remember for every punishable crime there is also a family that is suffering and needs our prayers.
> *Derek Smith*
> *Pack 942, Winston Salem, North Carolina*

➤ Do your best and always do what's right.
> *Den 3, Pack 97, Crescent Bay District, Santa Monica, California*

➤ Never Steal. It's better to be poor with a clean conscience than to be rich and guilty.
Thou shall not covet thy neighbor's dog.
> *Jordan Nunes, Boy Scout*

➤ Call your mother on Mother's Day and on her birthday.
> *David Petrocci*
> *Troop 757, Rockville, Maryland*

➤ Fulfill all family obligations before fulfilling personal ones.
> *Scout Patrick Michael McGovern*
> *Rockville, Maryland*

30 | Self Improvement

CUB AND BOY SCOUT
Rules of Civility for the 21st Century:

➤ Learn something new and do something that is hard for you each day.
Troop 1649
also Pack 31, Eau Claire, Wisconsin

➤ Do not make noise while others speak, and don't play music so loud that others have no choice but to listen.
Troop 334, Raleigh, North Carolina

➤ Choose the harder right way instead of the easier wrong way.
Also from Troop 334, Raleigh, North Carolina

➤ Gaze not upon images of hate and destruction but rather fill your heart and mind with the values of honor and integrity.
Den 9, Pack 289, Thompson's Station, Tennessee

➤ Do not watch television while doing homework. It interferes with concentration.
Do not pirate software or plagiarize (copy and call your own) information from books for reports.
Pack 1365, Lake Ridge, Virginia

➤ In order to love others, you must love yourself first.
Scouts of Den 4, Hawthorne Pack 1

➤ Learn from your mistakes. They can be some of your best teachers.
Bears/Den 3, Pack 36

➤ Try to learn what is being taught to you even if it doesn't interest you, because all information has value.
Troop 402, Jersey City, New Jersey
In the 21st century we will constantly be inundated with "infomercials" and all different types of information, not necessarily correct information, or infor-

mation with "strings attached." It will be a great challenge to sort out all this information, put it to the best use, or discard it.

➤ The accumulation of money and wealth are not necessarily the same.
> *Tall Grass District of Des Plaines Valley Council, Chicago, Illinois*

➤ Continue to read and learn throughout life. Keep your life pointed spiritually in the right direction. Also, learn to say no to temptations of life.

> *Pack 3400, Kreamer, Pennsylvania*

Lead us not into Temptation: to include alcohol abuse, drugs, illicit and unprotected sex, accepting a dare at the "extreme" limits of safety, and may the Lord deliver us from evil. —The Lord's Prayer

Mount Vernon—
George Washington's Home

GEORGE WASHINGTON came to live at Mt. Vernon after his older brother, Lawrence, died. He leased the mansion and farm from Lawrence's widow in 1754.

Five years later, George married Martha D. Custis and moved to Mount Vernon. When his sister-in-law died in 1761, George inherited the property. He and Martha added to the house as they lived there. When they needed more space, they added to the big house.

Mount Vernon first became the homestead for the Washington family when George's great grandfather, John Washington, began building in 1674.

George and Martha lived at Mount Vernon before he became the first President of the new United States of America. They lived there after he served as President.

Joseph Kukolla
Webelos Den 12, Pack 520, Indianapolis, Indiana

From The Mount Vernon Ladies' Association:

IT HAS BEEN A REAL PLEASURE for the staff of Mount Vernon and the Vice Regents to work with Henry Wheelwright on this very special project—*Rules of Civility for the 21st Century.*

George Washington penned his 110 *Rules of Civility* when he was a boy (the same age as many Scouts of today). These *Rules* were invaluable in establishing Washington's remarkable character and his moral and social leadership throughout his life.

In 1999, Mr. Wheelwright's inspiration culminated in a once-in-a-lifetime camporee at Mount Vernon for several thousand Scouts. Thousands of modern rules of etiquette and manners from Scouts around the country were presented as part of the Salute to George Washington. Many thousands of brochures reacquainted Scouts across the country with George Washington and pointed out how critical our First President's boyhood values were in the formation of this great country of ours. Mr. Wheelwright drew attention to the principles and civility that meant so much to George Washington, and made this information available to youngsters through Mount Vernon. These same standards are even more important and relevant today.

The Mount Vernon Ladies' Association depends on patriots such as Mr. Wheelwright to help us bring the message of George Washington's character and leadership to Americans of every age. When the federal and state governments turned down John Augustine Washington's offer to sell them Mount Vernon, a dynamic group of women took up the cause to preserve this special place. As the first women's organization and preservation group in the United States, they have maintained this estate since 1858 without any government funds.

The Association is pledged to educate the public. Our primary way to do so is to preserve the home of George Washington and make it open to the public every day of the year. Washington most graciously

112

opened his home to guests and travelers all the time. We welcomed over 1,100,000 visitors in 1999 to include approximately 300,000 students. Once again we were number one in visitation in historical homes. We own and operate the Mount Vernon Inn, which offers award-winning dining and high quality retail gifts and reproduction items in support of the preservation of Mount Vernon and our mission to educate everyone about the legacies of George Washington. We also have over 350 volunteers without whom we could not have the incredibly active and successful events such as Hands-on History, Colonial Days and Scouting Months. Our Bicentennial in 1999 involved no less than 876 cities and towns across the country that earned the distinction of becoming George Washington Communities.

This publication is destined to become yet another highlight of our Bicentennial Year. We hope that this book can pass on these rules of behavior from children to children everywhere to help them cope with today's fast paced and frequently uncivil society. So many of this country's problems could be eased by respect for each other and just plain good manners—just simple courtesy, a smile, and a thank you. This book will pass this message to all Americans across this great country of ours.

Most gratefully,
Mrs. Robert E. Lee IV
Regent, 1996–1999

The End of the 20th Century at Mount Vernon:

In 1999:

- 1,115,843 people visited Mount Vernon. The highest number since the nation's 1976 bicentennial.

- 1,900,000 (approximate) hits were recorded at Mount Vernon's two internet sites during February.

- 297,916 students visited Mount Vernon. The Highest in Mount Vernon's history.

- 26,580 hours were donated by members of Mount Vernon's Volunteer Program.

- 876 communities representing all 50 states became an official George Washington Bicentennial Community. Each Community planned four or more activities relating to Washington, at least one of which was a public event.

- 60,000 new commemorative George Washington $5 gold coins issued by the U.S. mint were sold. The proceeds of almost $2 million dollars will be applied toward the new George Washington Educational Center at Mount Vernon.

Income from visitors' use of food service and the gift shop will support the construction of three new facilities to enhance the educational experience of visiting George Washington's home in the 21st century.

A new orientation center featuring a large format film will bring Washington's personality to life. The museum will showcase important portraits, furniture, china, manuscripts and books related to Washington and his family. Most importantly, the George Washington Educational Center will use every current technological tool available to communicate Washington's extraordinary leadership in every walk of life. Visitors will be transported from a wilderness explored by a young George Washington to bloody battlefields to crowded halls of government. Every aspect of the Washington story will be told in a most authentic fashion.

Estimated cost of construction and implementing outreach programs—$60 million.

Proceeds from the sale of this book, whether sold by Mount Vernon or otherwise, will benefit Mount Vernon.

Scout Salute to George Washington

ON DECEMBER 14, 1999 at high noon bells tolled across America, books about George Washington were introduced to schools and libraries, letters to the editor appeared in newspapers concerning Washington's legacy to our nation, and trees were planted to commemorate the 200th anniversary of George Washington's death. Cub and Boy Scouts also gathered together to salute and honor George Washington and perpetuate his legacy. They submitted their "Rules of Civility" for the future, just as George Washington did when he was a youngster.

It is currently popular for "revisionist" historians to write salacious and derogatory fiction about our Founding Fathers. The entertainment industry (movies and television) relies on rumors spread by enemies, innuendo, imagination, and unsubstantiated "findings" for the sensationalism necessary to discredit the leaders of our new democratic republic 200 years ago, which is now the envy of the world.

At the end of the 20th century, a century in which millions of young American men and boys gave their lives in wars around the world to protect the freedoms and liberties written into our Constitution, the framers of this constitution are now treated with scorn, ridicule, and uncivil contempt. Until quite recently, George Washington, our first President and Commander-in-Chief of a small ragtag army that won our independence from the British was held in the highest esteem all across our country.

While Illinois is known as the "Land of Lincoln," George Washington is still regarded as the "Father of our Country." Consider that when the rising sun touches American soil it is in Washington County, Maine. When the sun sets on the continental United States of America, it sets on the only state named for our first president. The highest mountain in the northeastern United States is Mount Washington. A road named for George Washington runs through Key West, Florida, the southernmost point of the continental United States. All across America, this man's name is ascribed to

- 7 mountains
- 8 streams
- 9 colleges and universities
- 10 lakes
- 33 counties
- 121 towns and villages
- countless streets, schools, and monuments.

Washington, District of Columbia, is the capital of our great country, and the Washington monument is the tallest building in our nation's capital.

Many books are available about George Washington that document his life, military genius, diplomacy, and character. There is no doubt his attention to "Rules of Civility" as a boy contributed to his character and leadership later in life. Because his father died when he was eleven, boys living in single parent homes can better relate to him and share his anxieties about the future and the future for his family. He was a man of faith who prayed regularly. When he was inaugurated as our first president, he added "So help me God!" before bending over to kiss the bible. From the eulogy of Congressman Henry Lee—friend, colleague in war, neighbor in peace, and father of General Robert E. Lee: "first in the hearts of his countrymen, he was second to none in the humble and endearing scenes of private life; pious, just, humane, temperate, and sincere, uniform, dignified and commanding, his example was all the more edifying to all around him as were the effects of that example lasting." Civility personified.

So on November 6, 1999, approximately 2,000 Boy Scouts and 300 scout leaders participated in a three-day "Once in a Lifetime" Camporee at Mount Vernon sponsored by the National Capital Area Council of the Boy Scouts of America and organized by the Mount Vernon Ladies' Association to "Salute George Washington." Each Scout was expected to help draft the Boy Scout Rules of Civility for the 21st Century by working individually or as a team to draft ten modern rules of civility to be delivered to Mount Vernon as part of the "Salute."

From 400 pages of submitted rules of civility by Scouts from around the country, Scouts attending the Mount Vernon Encampment were asked to enter an Official Ballot for the three best rules of civility for the 21st century out of approximately 4,000. Amidst all the commemorative activities, tours, and parades, this was asking a lot from youngsters, considering the thousands of submitted rules and the duplications and variations of certain rules. It would also be tempting for Scouts to vote for their own rules and rules from their own pack or unit. Attending Scouts were from the regional National Capital Area Council; so it would be easy for voting scouts and their buddies to overweight certain precepts. Any obvious collusion is taken into consideration.

The most noteworthy rules are included throughout this book. The most popular rules follow. Please note that votes for similar rules are combined, and with so many choices, more than five scattered votes for any one rule carry considerable weight.

- Follow the Ten Commandments.
- Follow the Golden Rule.
- Treat nature with the utmost respect, striving to follow Scouting's "Leave no Trace" guidelines for outdoor activities.
- If someone is in need, try to help him/her—such as a handicapped or elderly person.
- Listen to others as if you were speaking.
- Be considerate—Don't take batteries out of the remote and put them in the Game Boy.
- Never breathe on anyone when you haven't brushed your teeth.
- Don't smack your food.
- Respect your elders, and above all—Respect yourself.
- Don't spit in front of girls, and don't throw frogs on them!

Boy Scout Troop 1 from Southern Maryland submitted the most

rules as a unit (135 precepts) for the camporee. The most popular of these submissions, as voted by the boys, are as follows:

- Wear your clothes right.
- Don't snack before meals.
- Don't prance around.

(My Maryland friend and Scoutmaster Jack Fenwick, whose son is an Eagle Scout, has informed me that this has to do with an aversion to marching.)

- Two ears and one mouth. Use them in that proportion.
- Don't diss on your Scoutmaster or your elders.

A final haunting submission from a solitary scout—

- When you grow up to be a parent, don't become a control freak.

Scout Submissions:

At the Salute to George Washington Camporee at Mount Vernon, Virginia, most of the proposed rules of civility submissions came from Maryland.

The most submissions from individual scouts came from

- Neshannock Township, Pennsylvania
- Lavergne, Tennessee
- Winston Salem, North Carolina

After Maryland, the states with the highest number of submitted Rules of Civility for the 21st Century:

2) Pennsylvania

3) New Jersey

4) Tennessee

5) California

6) North Carolina

7) Texas

Acknowledgements

I AM GREATLY INDEBTED to Michael Quinn of the Mount Vernon Ladies' Association of the Union, who is now at Montpelier. It was his idea to go to the Scouts, which he did so successfully. Without his efforts, there would not have been the large regional camporee at Mount Vernon—"A Once-in-a-Lifetime Sleepover" according to *Mount Vernon: Yesterday, Today, and Tomorrow.* More importantly, he convinced the National Capital Area Council of the Boy Scouts of America to invite Scout Units and Scouts across the nation to join the Salute to George Washington. Not only did thousands of rules of civility along with commemorative items pour in, but George Washington and all he stood for was reintroduced across our country by America's youngsters for this important anniversary . . . and perpetuated.

Not only did many Scout leaders roll up their sleeves to bring this about, but many volunteers and staff from The Mount Vernon Ladies' Association as well. We should not forget the extensive efforts of Den Mothers nationally to produce thoughtful submissions from so many young Cub Scouts. Considerable work was done to disseminate information to the Scouts, besides planning and implementing the memorable Salute to George Washington. I would like to especially thank Cathy Johns at Mount Vernon for her cheerful helpfulness all around. Civility in action. Also a special nod to my friend Carew Lee, Past Regent of the Mount Vernon Ladies' Association, for her support, and encouragement.

On the editorial side, Ellen McCallister Clark, who is Public Service Librarian at the Society of the Cincinnati Headquarters in Washington, D.C., has been most gracious and forthcoming with information and research. If you wish to research George Washington and literature about him, this is an excellent place to go. As to the Scouts, a tip of the hat to Eagle Scout William E. Worrall II and his dad for their insights and information. Finally, appreciation goes to John T. Phillips, II, Historian and Publisher of Goose Creek Productions. Publisher-to-Publisher and Editor-to-Editor insights are helpful and fruitful.

About the Editor

HENRY C. WHEELWRIGHT has developed, edited, and published over 45 outdoor, environmental, and natural history books for Stone Wall Press, Inc. since 1972. Prior to this and after graduating from the University of Virginia, he taught English Composition at the Fay School in Southboro, Massachusetts to 5th, 6th, and 7th grade boys. He lives on a small farm near The Plains, Virginia, with his wife, three children, and many animals.

FROM THE END of the 19th century:

> ". . . and so there ain't nothing more to write about, and I am rotten glad of it, because if I'd a knowed what a trouble it was to make a book I wouldn't a tackled it and aint't agoing to no more. But I reckon I got to light out for the Territory ahead of the rest, because Aunt Sally she's going to adopt me and sivilize me and I can't stand it. I been there before."
>
> (THE ADVENTURES OF HUCKLEBERRY FINN,
> *Mark Twain—New York: Charles L. Webster & Co. 1885*)

Notes

To the brave new 21st century:

> "Far from being oppressive, controlling, or constricting, the manners, instincts, and virtues we recognize in decent, considerate human beings—in the case of males, the manners, instincts, and virtues we associate with being a 'gentleman'—are liberating. To educate, humanize, and civilize a boy is to allow him to make the most of himself."
>
> (THE WAR AGAINST BOYS, HOW MISGUIDED FEMINISM IS HARMING OUR YOUNG MEN, *Christina Hoff Sommers—New York, London, Toronto, Sydney, Singapore: Simon & Schuster 2000)*

Civility Workshop

(Editor's Note: This "workshop" challenge is directed towards the individual, but it can be used in a group setting as well—schools, Scouts, camps, rainy day programs, etc. You, the reader, are encouraged to jot down your own answers or notations in the text for quick and appropriate reference. Too much space in this book would be wasted for lengthy essay questions, for which a notebook might be more appropriate.)

Section One

Devise your own Rules of Civility for the 21st Century.

Review the Scouts' and George Washington's Rules of Civility. At the end of each Section, write down your own "rule" to follow.

Give an example how you can use (implement) these rules in your personal life, to include your own new rule.

How can you help someone (friend, younger brother, etc.) who is lacking in these qualities?

Can you think of a new attribute of Civility? (Such as Accepting Responsibility?)

Please provide at least one "rule" or example of this "civility" in action.

Give a practical example of how you can put each Civility Section to work in your own life. (Example: Table Manners—If your mother [or wife] has had an especially tough day, volunteer to do the dishes before she asks you to.)

Section Two

This book has focused on George Washington as a civilized person. What other civilized person do you admire the most? And why?

From history:

In real life:

Describe an uncivilized (rude) person you know. What do you dislike the most about his behavior?

How can you tactfully (gently) convince him to improve his behavior (such as letting him know he's not funny, or not being fair)?

The Scouts recommend that you do a "good turn" daily. What new act of civility can you think of doing?

For a day?

For a week?

All the time without thinking about it?

Essay Questions

At an important outdoor ceremony at Stratford Hall, the Lee ancestral home in the Northern Neck of Virginia, General J. W. "Jack" Nicholson was present amongst a large audience to include many other candidates to become the new Executive Director for the mansion and grounds. Without warning the skies darkened and storm clouds suddenly gave way to rain. As others grabbed for raincoats or scurried away for shelter, without thinking, General Nicholson took off his great coat and without a word, placed it over the shoulders of a nearby lady whose lovely dress was beginning to become soaked by the rain. As it turned out, she was Head of the Search Committee. General Nicholson got the job.

An officer's code of conduct goes back hundreds of years. It starts with chivalry, and chivalry starts with civility.

Can you describe a simple act of civility that was rewarded far more than the act itself?

Can you think of your own little act of civility that was not rewarded, but still made you feel good inside?

A year later General Nicholson was attending a Memorial Day service luncheon reception on our lawn after speaking at our church. He was resplendent in his dress uniform, infantry blue, and decorations for service and valor. Our young deaf and mentally challenged son was enthralled and captivated by the man, his stature, and his uniform and brilliant decorations. As he moved closer, the child's plate of beef stew slipped and cascaded down General Nicholson's front and pants and onto his shoes. Without raising his voice, jumping back, or pushing the child away, he softly patted the boy on his shoulder, ignored the mess on his uniform, but raised his hand only so nobody would make a fuss to clean his uniform. He did not call any attention to himself, nor try to reprimand the child, who would have been devastated if he had been treated harshly—especially by his new idol.

Can you think of a simple act of civility that made someone else or others more comfortable, even at your own expense?

Sometimes civility takes courage. There may be no reward for an act of civility; you might become unpopular, and there might be danger in the undertaking. But the effects could be dramatic. This is the foundation from which true character is built.

The restored Union Railway Station in Washington, D.C. is not only the hub of transportation, it is a tourist Mecca of sorts for shops, restaurants, and even entertainment (movies). It can become quite crowded. In the Fast Food courtyard a small Japanese family were quietly trying to enjoy their meal. A table and a few chairs became available next to them. Some very tough-looking teenagers with body ornaments, ratty clothes, etc. rushed over to claim their new territory—barging ahead of people in line. Two plopped down in the available chairs, but two other boys began fighting over the remaining chair—tugging at it and using loud, vile language. Without hesitation, the young Japanese boy (about 9 years old) jumped up from his chair, took it over to the two fighters, bowed, and said quietly—"Please, please. Take my chair. I want you to have it." Even though one grabbed the little boy's chair without a word, they both quietly sat down and the group sullenly ate their food. The young boy returned to his family's table. His father moved slightly to share his seat with his son.

Can you reflect upon a courageous act of civility, or even a simple act of civility which was unpopular?

What were the consequences?

How has a simple act of civility improved a bad situation in your life?

Bonus Question

He who steals my purse steals trash. 'Tis something, nothing;
'Twas mine, 'tis his, and has been slave to thousands;
But he that filches from me my good name
Robs me of that which not enriches him,
And makes me poor indeed.

—*Othello,* by William Shakespeare

What do you say to someone who is trying to ruin another person's good name?

If you are the one being defamed, what can you do about it?

Advanced Civility Seminar

Part One

Your school has invited a guest speaker to give a talk. Your group either disagrees with his politics (perhaps a book he has written), or does not like the organization he represents or simply belongs to. They want to disrupt his talk and shout him down. Perhaps throw a pie or worse at him. What do you tell them?

Challenge the most "civilized" member of your group (volunteer?). The rest of the group describes or acts out a situation testing this person's "civility." (Dangerous driving, throwing a wild party when your parents are away from home, marking up or destroying public or abandoned property, etc.)

Discuss the response and analyze alternative actions (and their consequences).

Part Two

Create a new civility category such as *Sportsmanship.* Ask each member of your group to come up with a precept. Then ask the person to give some examples of this new precept in action. Examples:

Don't play dirty: hit from behind, trip, elbow or push, take a "cheap shot", see what you can get away with the referees.

Involve everyone on your team: encourage rooting and "talking it up", help weaker players, and help the coaches (round up equipment, work on the field, pass out schedule changes).

Respect your opponents: treat them as guests (not enemies) by making them comfortable at your field/facilities, drop to one knee when a person is hurt, help another player up, shake hands after the game, consider a team cheer for the other team. *And the umpires, referees:* don't use profane language on the field and don't get too upset when you get a bad call. Ask your parents not to yell at the refs.

Be a good loser as well as a good winner: Congratulate your opponents. Commend someone for a good play. Don't whine and complain and make excuses. Be happy with yourself for playing has hard and fairly as you could. Thank your coaches and even a Higher Power for the glory of the day.

A Sportsmanship Story:

My son Lee joined the Marshall A's Little League baseball team for 11–12 year olds. The infield and pitching were "pat" so Lee played outfield with most of the rest of the team. He was fast and good—field and bat. However, the team had a nice rule that everyone got to play; so Lee only got to play a couple of innings each game. T.J., on the other hand, was slow, not muscularly coordinated, and had trouble getting the bat around.

A couple of times in close games with runners in scoring position, T.J. would strike out on three or four pitches to kill a rally. Everyone was really good about it, but you could tell the kids were disappointed. They kind of avoided him.

"I stink!" he barked out in the dugout, kicking his glove.

"No you don't!" replied Lee. "You've got to believe in yourself. Come on, let's throw the ball." And from then on at practices, when the kids paired up to throw balls, shag flies, etc., you could find Lee working out with T.J.

The season wound down to the final inning of the final game of the league tournament. Score tied and up came T.J. He whiffed at the first two pitches but got a little piece of the third and beat out a nubber down the third base line. Up came Lee. The first pitch was low in the dirt. "Don't go!" yelled the first base coach. But T.J. took off and stole second base. Lee came around late on the next fastball and drove a liner into right field. T.J. scored to win the championship.

After the tumult and the shouting died, and Lee and I were walking back to the car, I said, "Lee, I don't care if you ever get another hit. I am so proud of you for working with that kid!" Lee grinned.

Can you think of an important element of civility in your life, as it relates to sportsmanship?

Part Three: Discussion Topics

Bullying

Bullying is often the most uncivil and humiliating and traumatic experience of childhood. This can be traced back to primeval societies, and the law of the jungle where the strong suppress or even stamp out the weak. Alpha males dominate various animal groups (such as baboon tribes) and are often the only ones to mate with the females. In our modern society, especially with youngsters, a big aggressive kid will torment or beat up a smaller and weaker kid. Other kids will team up with the bully to avoid being abused themselves. The bully will harass weaker, "different", and/or handicapped kids and make that person's life miserable. If the weaker child is smarter in class, this will provoke the bully and his cohorts even more.

With boys, bullying might start with teasing and name calling. This could escalate into physical pushing and tripping. Then marking up, damaging, or even destroying the targeted child's possessions. If the boy rats to a teacher or supervisor, this will cause him more trouble from the bully and his gang.

Have you ever been bullied? What did you do about it?

Have you seen another kid being bullied? What did you do about it?

If you didn't do anything, what did you want to do about it? What could you do?

What advice would you give to the child being bullied?

Bullying isn't just for boys. Just because a little girl isn't socked in the eye doesn't mean she isn't bullied by the other girls. The other girls can start with sarcasm and move to teasing. Then finally social ostracism (being excluded from conversation, activities, etc.)

What would you do about it?

Adolescence and "puberty" conjures up many images—curiosity, fascination, exploration, spin the bottle, doctor and nurse. Cross the line (wherever it is-often not far) and you are guilty of "sexual harassment", according to a 5–4 Supreme Court decision. Everybody gets sued. As Christina Hoff Sommers points out in her book *The War Against BOYS, How Misguided Feminism is Harming our Young Men* (Simon and Schuster, 2000)—"Children torment and humiliate one another for all sorts of reasons; sex is just one of dozens." She cites a U.S. Department of Education study that found 5.1% of males and 3.3% of female students (ages 12 to 19) had experienced "violent victimization at school."

Discuss different ways a youngster can be bullied/victimized. What can be done about it?

Bullying isn't just for kids either. Imposing your own philosophy or sexual politics on a naïve or unwilling captive audience (class) is a form of bullying as well. If you are a boy and don't want to dress up in girl's clothes or play with dolls or be forced to watch sexually graphic, objectionable film, what can you and/or your parents do about it?

Christina Hoff Sommers adds that youngsters "need strong moral guidance" and a school environment that does not "tolerate egregious meanness or gross incivility, whether sexual or nonsexual."

Do you know someone who is overly bossy—always telling people to do things? Never satisfied or appreciative when they are done. What can you and/or others do about it?

Do you know of someone who won't let others finish a conversation, or even a sentence without jumping in with some snide remark or to change the subject to suit themselves? What can you and/or others do about it?

Words

> "Sticks and stones may break my bones, but words will never hurt me!"
>
> —*Old Saying*

Not as we enter the 21st century. No matter how we communicate with each other, by word of mouth or through the most advanced technology, we must use words. Language changes, but the English language (paradoxically the most universal language in the world) is in decline—or rather the acceptable use of it. Fewer words are acceptable (those clearly understood by most people) and many more are unacceptable (found offensive by anyone, no matter how ignorant). Frustration mounts. One of the rudest (most uncivil) comments someone can make is "Oh, shut up!" A definite conversation stopper.

I could see the handwriting on the wall a few years ago. At a prestigious small liberal arts college in Vermont a senior used the word "niggardly" (correctly) in an English composition. The professor called her in to his study and, trembling with rage, handed back her "F" paper and admonished her with "Don't you ever use that word again!" She had not used the word in any racist way and was flabbergasted and devastated. She was also upset he might give her a bad recommendation to keep her out of graduate school. As the 20th century came to a close, a bright young man used the word correctly and innocently in a communication and was immediately fired from the District of Columbia government. (Later reinstated after the press got hold of it.)

How do you determine what words somebody might find offensive? Can you ever use these words again?

Fighting words—We all know them. They start with "fraidy cat!" and "sissy" and evolve into disparaging personal remarks that are offensive but perhaps mildly amusing to others: "shorty," "tubby," etc. I grew up on a farm in Maryland (now they are selling houses, not steers). One farm hand called his younger brother "porky" and the younger boy heaved his pitchfork at him. Fortunately he missed, but he delivered a clear message. These words can brand a child for life.

Discuss "fighting words." Why do some people deliberately provoke others with them, and how do you put a stop to it?

Freedom of expression? Not if you fall out of a canoe in Michigan and swear up a blue storm, which offends a family with small children in a boat upriver. You go to court, are found guilty, pay a fine, and perhaps do community service. Civility and civilized behavior and common courtesy triumph—but at what price? Discuss.

On the doorstep of the 21st century are the politically correct police, stamping out all language that is in the least bit offensive to anyone, especially females and "minorities" in the broadest sense of the word (except white males). Perhaps the penultimate is the "unacceptable language" officials at Stockport College near Manchester, England who have banned about forty words (so far). According to a front page article (June 13, 2000) in the *Washington Times*, these include—

- Lady and gentleman (unwanted class implications)
- History and postman (sexist)
- Crazy, mad, and manic (might offend people with mental health problems)
- Queer or cripple (may only be used where gay or disabled people have "reclaimed them")
- Chairman, manmade, etc. (sexist)

Stockport officials have made it a "condition of service and admission" that students and employees follow this policy so as not to offend various population groups. For whatever it is worth, I have heard that the early English suffix—"man" is gender neutral; so we don't have to fuss with hundreds of words. Don't try to explain this to the officials at Stockport College, who are standing firm on their new policy of word policing. Critics are pointing out the absurdity of banning ordinary words that are used every day by ordinary people. One suggested the college change its mailing address from Manchester to "Personchester".

At a time when we need a larger vocabulary to better define a concept, idea, creative work, technology, etc. we are clashing with limitations imposed by special interest groups that are concerned that someone might be offended (even through a misunderstanding). More and more words are owned by companies for commercial purposes. Discuss.

A civilized person constantly seeks to improve himself (or herself), his condition, his language, and how he gets along with others. How do you balance this without offending (even unintentionally) some other person, race, gender, sexual orientation, religion, nationality, etc.,etc.? This is one of the greatest challenges for civility in the 21st century.

Respect

Discuss the importance of **not** finding offensive a charitable comment or language that is not meant to offend you. Yet, how do you explain to a person that you are uncomfortable with his language, jokes, etc.? Is there a middle ground that will allow you both to communicate effectively with each other—without offending the other?

At the end of the 20th century, an "all-century" baseball team was honored in Yankee Stadium. Pete Rose was interviewed by a very confrontational NBC-TV commentator who pressed him on his prior gambling addiction and banishment from baseball. New York manager Joe Torre's reaction was that "we've lost sight of the word 'respect.' We deal too much in shock value."

Do you think the media has lost respect for athletes, politicians, and the people who are interviewed? Explain.

How would you balance respect with probing questions to elicit interesting or newsworthy answers?

Do you think professional athletes have lost respect for their coaches, the game, and the fans? Can this be turned around?

According to the French Jesuits of the 16th century, George Washington, and today's Scouts, civility begins with respect. And with Respect, we close this book. Respect—the alpha and omega of civility. Respectfully, it ends with you and me and how we tolerate, and "just get along" with everyone else in this ever-more-crowded neighborhood, global, and cyber universe of the 21st century.

Be happy with yourself, but delight in someone who is different. Enjoy an inner, civil peace, and let those who want to rush on by—well, just rush on by.

The Final Word(s) . . .

. . . should go to the Scouts—

➤ Be honest, courteous, trustworthy, responsible, kind to others, worship regularly.
> *Cub Pack 311*
> *Evansville, Indiana*

What final words can you think of to cere the importance of civility in your mind and heart, and to carry forward into the future?

Why America Is Free

by Hamburger, Fischer & Gravlin

208 pages, 140 full-color illustrations
Hardbound, $12.95
Published by the
Society of the Cincinnati
in cooperation with
The Mount Vernon Ladies' Association

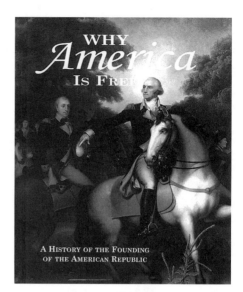

Why America Is Free instills an understanding and appreciation of the nature of American freedom through a dramatic re-telling of the heroic true story of George Washington and a new nation struggling for independence. Using the perspective of an ordinary citizen, *Why America Is Free* brings American history to life for young students and citizens.

In this unique account, traditional historical content is shared through the first-person account of Jedidiah Warwick, a fictitious 18th-century character. Jedidiah, a 9-year-old colonial farm boy in 1750, takes readers along as he grows up during the most dramatic and influential period in American history.

Order your copy of *Why America Is Free* and/or additional copies of *Rules of Civility for the 21st Century* for friends, Scouts, schools, or libraries.

- ✂ - - -

Please send me the following books:

_____ copies of *Why America Is Free* @ $12.95 each . . . . subtotal _____

_____ copies of *Rules of Civility for the 21st Century* @ $15.00 each . . subtotal _____

Shipping and handling ($3 for first book + $1 for each additional) . . . . subtotal_____

Total enclosed _____

Send to:

NAME _____

ADDRESS _____

CITY, STATE, ZIP _____

Make checks payable to:
Mount Vernon Ladies' Association.
Send coupon and payment to:
**George Washington's Mount Vernon,
Education Department, PO Box 110,
Mount Vernon, VA 22131**